Wilfred Cantwell Smith

Belief and History

University Press of Virginia

Charlottesville

Richard Lectures for 1974-75
University of Virginia

THE UNIVERSITY PRESS OF VIRGINIA
Copyright © 1977 by the Rector and Visitors
of the University of Virginia

First published 1977
First paperback printing 1985

Library of Congress Cataloging in Publication Data

Smith, Wilfred Cantwell, 1916-
   Belief and history.

   Includes bibliographical references and index.
   1.   Faith—Addresses, essays, lectures.
2. Belief and doubt—Addresses, essays, lectures.
3. Religion and language—Addresses, essays, lectures.
I. Title.
BV4637.S558   234'.2   76-50587
ISBN 0-8139-0670-9 (cloth); 0-8139-1086-2 (paper)

Printed in the United States of America

345357

Preface

The thesis of this book is radical. Accordingly, it is developed rather gradually; moreover, the substantiating data on which it rests are set forth at some length in elaborated notes and references.

At the level of historical fact, the thesis is quite simple and straightforward; and at that level, although new and somewhat surprising, it could doubtless be fairly readily recognized as cogent. A change in the meaning of terms has actually taken place; this can hardly be gainsaid. The implications of this, on the other hand, will be received with less unanimity. Some will find them exhilarating, liberating. Others may resist them, or find them unmanageable, so established in modern thinking have the results of the change firmly become, and so heavily pressured are moderns to read their new outlook back into the past. I am suggesting that when one looks carefully, one discovers that it was not there.

The idea that believing is religiously important turns out to be a modern idea. It has arisen in recent times, in ways that can be ascertained and demonstrated. I might almost sum up the implications of my thesis, as distinct from the thesis itself, by saying that a great modern heresy of the Church is the heresy of believing. Not of believing this or that, but of believing as such. The view that to believe is of central significance—this is an aberration.

Curiously, this heresy is shared not only by "believers" but by critics of the Church, by outsiders. Anti-religious thinkers have come to hold even more doggedly than theologians that believing is what religious people primarily do. To return to the historical level: whatever be the case to-day, it turns out to be wrong to suppose that this is what Christians have primarily done in the past, or have thought important to do. Traditionally, classically, their emphasis has in fact been elsewhere.

Nowadays any discussion of religious belief has to take note of the philosophy of religion of recent linguistic analysts, and accordingly our first chapter delves into that matter. Secondly, we observe the history of the English words "belief" and "believe", since these *words*, of course, *are* traditional; but they used to name something quite other than the propositionalist opinion to which they nowadays refer. Thirdly, we look at the Bible, suggesting that a concept of believing is not to be found in it.

The implications of the thesis are not here developed. If faith, rather than belief, be the fundamental religious category, as I hold that history shows, and that rationality demands, then the inter-relation between faith and belief becomes a crucial question. (This is so especially for those of us who are rationalists.) That question, however, is the topic of another volume.

I wish to thank those responsible for the Richard Lectures programme for their invitation to participate in that distinguished series; and the Department of Religious Studies at the University of Virginia, and especially its former and present chairman Professor David Harned, for their warm hospitality to Mrs. Smith and me during our visit to their charming campus. The honour of being appointed to the lectureship, the delight of being received in their midst, and the opportunity of working out these ideas, are all appreciatively acknowledged. I wish also to record my gratitude to the University Press of Virginia for understanding and patience in dealing with my unusual typescript.

WILFRED CANTWELL SMITH

Dalhousie and Harvard Universities

Contents

Belief and History

I. The Meaning
of Religious Statements
Comments on a Debate

THE HISTORIAN OF religion is embarked on a task that is, surely, bold. The endeavour to understand the religious life of a people—men's and women's orientations and aspirations, at their most intimate and profound, their societies' assumptions and cohesions, at their most subtle and pervasive; and much else—that endeavour is venturesome. It is still more venturesome when in addition one tackles the *history* of religion, attempting to discern all this in motion over the centuries: the sudden or gradual shifts; the unconscious reading of new meanings out of or into old symbols, or the adoption of new symbols perhaps to affirm quite new perceptions but at times also to carry afresh the old ones; or the development of new emphases, new patterns, or even new systems, in slow or swift processes that we hold to be not unintelligible but usually find also to be not obvious. And there is a yet more audacious step when one aspires, further, to be a *comparativist* historian: seeing two or more of the conspicuously diverse developments in relation to each other, attempting to discern and to formulate traditions' similarities and differences—for both of which precision turns out to be surprisingly elusive—, or to apprehend their historical interactions and mutual impingement as well as their distinctness.

All this is admittedly bold. The question is, is it not overly bold? Is the aspiring scholar in this field not, in fact, pretentious? As one of my predecessors at Harvard once remarked, rather devastatingly: Before we compare two things, we should know at least one of them.[1] Yet here are we aspiring, not only to know, but also to understand. Does anyone understand religion; and specifically perhaps faith in a form other than his own? Does anyone understand human history, and the processes by which one situation becomes another (that word "becomes" is so disarmingly simple!)? Is anyone truly able to compare historical developments of varying communities, in the sense of comprehending two or more in their mutual relation, and their mutual estrangement?

To me it is evident that the comparativist historian of religion is in a field of scholarship where it is in principle impossible fully to attain one's goal. Nonetheless I continue to work at it, with increasing conviction and indeed excitement; and to encourage others to enter it, urging on them that by doing so they may learn something richly rewarding, and may contribute something of deep significance to the intellectual life of our age: indeed, something requisite. Our task seems forbidding, yet is not merely delightful but imperative. How so?

An answer is that no serious understanding of man but must begin with an awareness of, even a focus upon, his subtlety and complexity, his transcending grandeur and bathos, his mystery—and his involuted role in this process as both knower and known. To recognize that we transcend our own and each other's comprehension is the first step towards any authentic apprehension.

It is indeed bold to harbour pretensions about having grasped the religious dimension of human life, or the historical, or the comparative, so deep and elusive are these, so intractable within our ideational nets. Yet it is even bolder, more foolhardy, more pretentious, to make any pronouncement on the human condition these days omitting these considerations. What little we know in these transcending realms is indeed tentative; yet the value of that little seems perhaps confirmed when it is confronted with judgements that would appear to ignore these distinctive qualities and contexts of everything human.

All this is prolegomenon to our topic for this chapter, and this book. The question of how to understand religious faith, and more specifically, how to understand religious belief, is a haunting one; and I have wondered whether a comparativist historian of religion might perhaps make some contribution to a discussion of it. He begins aware that he does not know enough, and in addition does not understand enough, properly to tackle so momentous a human problem. If he nonetheless pitches in, it is perhaps because he has decided to be tentative without being intimidated.

Intimidated he might well have been, for he finds the field apparently already occupied by others. For some time now in the English-speaking world the question of the nature and meaning of religious belief has been chiefly in the hands of a group calling themselves philosophers of religion with a special concern for language. The movement began with a fulsome rejecting of all talk about God; insofar as there has been a response, it has come largely from Christians philosophically oriented, some of whom seem disappointingly acquiescent in the terms of debate as postulated. A rather large literature has been generated on the issue by these two.

Two basic considerations would seem then to apply, to anyone who would venture into this realm. The first is that a preliminary requirement might presumably be that he familiarize himself with that literature. Secondly, however, and over against this, many on the outside looking in find themselves quite ill at ease with all this. They feel that something has gone seriously awry with the whole recent discussion, it apparently having got off on a wrong track, wandering into a wilderness—where, perhaps wrongly, they feel it hardly worthwhile to follow.

In the debate, some have reported religious statements meaningless. To a person of faith, of course, but also to an historian, that sounds unlikely; to a comparativist, preposterous. How can two clearly different statements both be meaningless—statements that have been historically consequential in mighty, and divergent, ways? Yet the kind of meaning that the other side of the debate sometimes defends, also seems somehow unsatisfying. Perhaps it is time to suggest from a different perspective that another line altogether may prove more promising for an understanding of religious belief.

The problem, as I see it, has the same three facets that I have listed. Both sides—both hostile philosophers, and philosophic theologians—seem to have tended to underplay the historical aspect of the issues being canvassed; to ignore the comparative; and at times almost to be by-passing the religious—at least, the more profoundly religious, or faith—aspect. The protagonists will doubtless counter that in any contribution that I may presume to proffer in these talks, I shall in turn be displaying my insensitivity to the philosophic. I have decided to run that risk. Or, rather than calling it a risk, I am in fact hopeful that my venturesomeness may be repaid by my being alerted through criticism to my deficiencies in that realm. Matters of religious believing undoubtedly involve philosophic questions (even if it not be so obvious to some as it appears to be to others that current philosophic moods have grasped them aright). Equally, however, they involve religious, of course, and historical and comparativist questions; as we shall be noting. Indeed, I hope to show that these are involved in a compelling, ineluctable, way; and to suggest, in a helpful way.

My own incapacity to effect a synthesis of my historian's view with the current philosophic, stems at least in part from lack of serious acquaintance with the positions from which mine differs; a lack to which I have already pleaded guilty. Yet that failure of familiarity stems, in its turn, in part from the radical divergence between us. The fact is that on and off for a couple of decades now I have on various occasions looked into the growing literature, but must confess that I have never managed to stick with it. It has tended to strike me, frankly, as from the point of view of my concerns rather superficial, and irrelevant. The historian overhears a debate, but it sounds too uninteresting to command full attention. As I study the religious life of Muslims (as I have been doing now for almost forty years), or of Hindus (with increased seriousness for the past decade), or of others, largely through considering their spoken and written words; and as I reflect on the panorama of man's religious life and its history, my own community's and others', across the centuries and around the globe, and attempt to articulate a conceptual scheme that will make theoretical sense of that panorama; I find that the observations of such critical linguistic philosophers of religion as I come across let us say, from Ayer to Nielsen—do not seem much to impinge on anything that I am doing. They are not merely not helpful; they seem not even pertinent.

Moreover, so far as I am aware, this situation of mine is quite general. Among my fellow historians of religion, whether of individual traditions one by one or as comparativists surveying the broader scene, I know few, if any, who find the critical analysis of modern-day linguistic philosophers of religion of interest or significance for their work.[2]

Something calling itself a philosophy of science that proved irrelevant or boring to historians of science, studying scientific developments over the centuries, would seem odd. This might not matter decisively provided that the theories proffered were serviceable to the practising scientist in his laboratory. If, however, an interpretation of science had bearing neither for the careful observer nor for the practitioner, one would feel it strange. Critical linguistic philosophy of religion seems to fall into some such case: it does not illuminate empirical studies, either of religious movements in general or of the history of religious belief; and religious persons themselves keep protesting that they have been misunderstood. An unkind outsider might allow himself to be surprised that those calling themselves philosophers of language should know so few languages, and so little linguistics (especially cultural), and that those calling themselves empiricists should be so unrelievedly ratiocinative, their disquisitions unanchored in the observational data of the religious or linguistic history of the race.

These remarks refer primarily to the negative side of the debate, by which the tone seems to have been set: a sustained series of accusations that "religious statements" are meaningless, irrational, or simply false. The prevailing mood seems to be that of a proselytizing mission or assault[3] more than of a genuine inquiry.

The response within the field, chiefly from certain Christian thinkers, has been of course important, even impressive. Yet here again, given the belligerence of the attack, the movement has tended to be more defensive than constructive. In particular, given the great concern to disparage or to justify belief, or some particular belief, there is perhaps room for a contribution proffered rather towards understanding it. I wonder whether either side, or indeed practising Christians, and for that matter Jews or Hindus and others, will in turn find the views that I here set forth any less off the point. Let us see.

Anyway, my thesis is that with much of the current dispute on religious statements one has a certain malaise for three reasons: that it has failed to reckon with their religious quality, their historical quality, and their comparative contexts. Let us look at each in turn.

I

If we start with the religious, I could be asked what I mean by that; and I should be tempted to answer that I mean, virtually, the human quality—except that historicity also is an inherent human characteristic, as is also cultural variety. I would say, then, that by "religious" I mean personal, so long as one is not so individualistic still as to imagine that *personal* is over against social. On the contrary: the counterpart of social is individual, the counterpart of personal is impersonal. An individual becomes a person in society; and a society becomes a community by being personal, just as it becomes dehumanized, a juxtaposition or congeries of alienations, by being impersonal. By "religious", then, I mean nothing mysterious; except insofar as the human is mysterious. I do insist that to understand persons one must not reduce them to something less; one must recognize what they do and say as fully human, fully personal. Linguistic philosophy has—almost deliberately—failed to do justice, even to try to do justice, to religious (and other) statements as personal, human; when this is what they primarily and essentially are. Even when talking about the natural world, religious statements are about that world humanly. Every religious statement is a statement about man. If it is a statement also about something else, then it is a statement about man and that thing in interrelation (which is not so obviously a weakness as some may have supposed).

In fact, the concern of this school with "religious language", and indeed the very focus of modern linguistic philosophy generally on language, seem a function of that philosophy's incapacity to deal with persons and the personal. Aping what it considers to be science, which is oriented to the material world, it seems unable to think about (let alone, to interpret adequately) what is not an object (and persons are misunderstood if they are thought of as objects; so is the personal). Accordingly, faced with something human, such as the religious, these thinkers cannot proceed until they have objectified it. This they seize upon language as a device to enable them to do. A sentence, once it is uttered, stands halfway between the objective world and the world of persons; there is a danger, if it be treated in isolation, of one's coming up with half-truths about man.

Any philosophy of language is awry that considers language, or any instance of it, in and of itself; as if it could be dealt with apart from the human beings with whom it is involved. To treat anything human without focusing on its human quality must be suspect.

An understanding, then, of the meaning of religious belief, I am suggesting, will escape being radically inadequate and jejune in proportion as it is sensitive to the profundity, the elusive quality, the complexity, of the religious quality of human life, or simply of the personal quality of human life.

Our human life transcends our human apprehension (of course!); and in its religious quality most of all.

Nonetheless, one is not stumped. We have gone far towards understanding this quality, this transcendence, and anyone can understand it better than he yet does, if he work at it. Neither should one fool oneself that one has arrived, when one is only on one's way, nor should one fail to set out upon that way. No interpretation of a religious belief need be taken very seriously that does not elucidate it as a belief but also elucidate it as religious.

This means in part that the interpretation of it should enable us to apprehend man better than we had previously been able to do: to see better than before how subtle man is, how grand, how diverse, how wretched. The student of religious history is engaged in the task of discovering, and of making intelligible to others, how each of the data of man's religious life here or there across the centuries and across the globe constitutes one more clue for our deepening awareness of the incomprehensible, yet herein manifest, humanity of man.

One need not like everything that one sees. Man's sinfulness as well as his glory always transcends our grasp; and both are constantly being more richly documented than we realized any given yesterday. Of any religious belief, an interpretation—by a philosopher of religion or by anybody else—that fails to take seriously its religiousness and to exegete that, is trivial. The historian of religion finds no belief statement that does not open up one more window, large or small, gracious or grotesque, on the religious reality of both man and the universe. Or at the very least this much we may affirm: that for a belief to be religious means that it is linked in some fashion to faith, so that the ascertaining of its meaning involves at least the ascertaining and explicating of that link; and ultimately the illuminating of that faith.

I would have much sympathy with someone studying Hindu, Buddhist, Islamic, Chinese, Jewish, or Christian life, who reported himself overwhelmed by the richness and power of a given religious statement, finding it to mean more than he could understand. In contrast, one might have little sympathy, and could be tempted to have little patience even, with one who announced blandly that it had no meaning. Even with the former, however, a little effort should dissuade him from giving up. Although in the end perhaps every religious statement (and not only the *Mahavakya*[4] "Great Sayings") means more than we can understand, none means more than we can begin to understand. These things are as both Chuang-tzu and K'ung Fu-tzu spoke of them as being: namely, that this side even of infinity is near us, even if the far side be beyond our grasp (or there be no far side). "I know how to get to [its stupendous spaces] ", said Chuang-Tzu, speaking of the realm of Tao; "but I do not know where they end".[5] "It is to be found everywhere, yet it is a secret" is the Confucian counterpart: "The simple intelligence of ordinary men and women of the people may understand something of Tao; but in its utmost reaches there is something that even the wisest and holiest of men cannot understand".[6]

These, by the way, are two religious statements of which it would seem to me rather pitiful for anyone either not to understand the meaning in part, or to suppose that he had understood it totally. As a matter of fact, however, I am not sure that this quality does not characterize all human discourse. Surely it is the case with so simple a statement, for instance, as "This is an apple", to say nothing of so ramifying a one as "She loves him". Anyone who pretended fully to understand the meaning of either of these, would surely be wrong. One may imagine persons with no understanding of one or other of them, or of both; yet, equally surely, would this not be recognized as a failure on those persons' part, from which in principle they could, and from which it would be hoped that they might, be rescued by learning? To know nothing about apples, or to suppose that one knows all about them, is sad. How much sadder, in the case of love.

I have come across no religious statement anywhere whose meaning did not illuminate for me something about man (not simply the men or women who made it, and those who have cherished it, but about man in general); and usually about man's relation to the world. For this, one must have, perhaps, some understanding of human faith; given that understanding, from particular religious statements one can learn much. Perhaps to fail to appreciate the religious quality of human life may lead to an insensitivity to the meaning of religious language; but one should realize that to fail to appreciate this quality of human life is drastically to misunderstand both humankind and the universe in which we live.

What I am saying implies, perhaps, that a minimal understanding of faith is prerequisite to understanding a religious statement. Yet that understanding of faith can *begin* by being quite minimal indeed: perhaps simply the recognition that persons are not things or machines. Once one is launched on this exciting venture, then each new statement from around the world that one minimally appreciates enhances that basic understanding, so that the next statement, in turn, appears more meaningful, or the more readily meaningful; and so it increasingly goes.

This question of understanding man as the focus is, I have increasingly come to feel, basic. Sir Alfred Ayer, in his recent Gifford Lectures[7] and elsewhere, asserts that a metaphysical system or conceptual scheme must have explanatory value, meaning that it should explain observable facts. Yet as he proceeds it becomes quickly quite evident that by "observable facts" he means those of the natural world; and he explicitly refers to the natural sciences as our only reliable source of knowledge. This provides, I think, a clue to his whole outlook, and to his manifest failures in our realm. For the natural sciences take note of, are interested in, explain, the world of physical nature only. If that is all that you are interested in, fine (though even so, you have to be conditioned by modern Western culture to be interested in it "objectively", apart from several of man's other involvements with it). If, on the other hand, you happen to be interested in your fellow man, then with this sadly limited world-view you are in trouble. If philosophically you have dogmatized that both truth and meaning lie only in that objectivist scientific realm, not at all in inter-personal relations, as we shall elaborate a little in our next chapter, then your troubles are severely compounded.

Even a second-rate metaphysical theory has more explanatory

value than does Ayer's, for making sense of the observed facts of personal life, of human love and courage and loyalty, of the beauty of nature; and even of that human passion to understand the physical world truly that is science. Not that I am satisfied with second-rate metaphysical theories! We cannot to-day let even the first-rate geniuses of the past do our thinking for us; though from all the great classics, from Aristotle to Chu Hsi, and from Plato and especially Plotinus to Samkara and Rumi, I myself have found much that is of explanatory value for understanding human history, which is fundamentally religious history. A theory explicitly oriented on the other hand primarily to things, and that has proven so distorting of personal life, both individual and corporate, is hardly the last word.

Let me put that less belligerently. My suggestion is that one reason why some modern logic and linguistic analysis have proven inept at understanding religious discourse, is that they have set themselves up as a philosophy of natural sciences at a time when that science is oriented not to man, and is oriented even to the natural world in a fashion that for the first time on a grand scale in human history considers that natural world in explicit disjunction from man. It even boasts of this; its concept of objectivity postulates impersonalism, and holds that true knowledge shall be considered to have been attained only if the relation of the person to what is known be eliminated. Small wonder then if religion is deemed untrue, and religious sentences not to convey knowledge.

With a different view, do religious statements become at once lucidly intelligible? Lest I seem pretentiously to claim so, or myself to have neglected the dimension of transcendence, let me close this section of my presentation by calling attention to a religious position that I frankly admit to not understanding. It, too, may prove instructive. At least it will illustrate how an Ayer and I differ in our approaches to something that we do not understand.

In the Islamic, but to some extent in the Hindu and to a lesser degree the Buddhist, fields I may perhaps report that I, and certainly various friends among my colleagues and teachers and students, have begun to see the point, to grasp the meaning, of such religious statements as come to our attention, however alien these might at first blush seem to our quite different ways of thinking, and however comparable they might appear to be to propositions nearer home that hostile linguistic analysts find vacuous. To understand these is our professional academic business; and I am claiming that we have made some progress towards that goal, and know how to proceed to make more. In the case of ancient Egypt, however, my own studies have been superficial and unsustained. I am impressed by the massive elegance and exquisite sumptuousness of ancient-Egyptian art and especially architecture. I am impressed by two thousand years of pre-Ptolemaic Egyptian history, and by the order that its people attained or created in political life, in mathematics, and in technological achievements. So far as their religious life is concerned, which permeated and suffused all their other accomplishments, I am impressed by it, too: impressed by the power and elegance of their imagination, and the close correlation between it and their most practical operations. If one discriminates between the aesthetic and the artistic, as referring respectively to the appreciation and to the construction of beauty, its recognition and its creation, then we may say that the ancient Egyptians perceived the world artistically. Or, if we shift to seeing the human relation to transcendence not as quest so much as as response, then we may say that the universe appeared to the ancient Egyptians artistically. It is an entrancing question as to why it presented itself so to them more than it does to us. The religious aspect of their life is the evidence for us that this happened; and shows us the mode and manner of it. The data stand as to some degree the result, and to some degree the cause, of this artistry, of perception or of presentation.

Now this whole realm is rewardingly rich. Yet for the moment I wish simply to single out one observation of theirs that, frankly, I do not understand. They held that the sky is a cow.[8] Actually it was a good deal more complicated than that; with reference to a particular goddess[9] and much else. But leaving subtleties aside, we are faced with this remark, and are challenged to say what they meant. Now the ancient Egyptians were highly intelligent people, highly practical people, highly observant people. Furthermore, we must remember that the weather in the lower Nile valley is exceptionally clear, indeed brilliant. It is not as if they lived always under storm-clouds or dense pollution, so that they could not see the sky and were simply speculating about what it might be like behind some impenetrable screen. They saw the sky day after day much more clearly than you or I have ever regularly done; and they probably had seen more cows than some of us.

Now you and I know very well that the sky is not a cow. One possible conclusion might then be that the ancient Egyptians were simply wrong when they said that it was. This would be essentially the position of an Ayer, and of many a nineteenth-century Christian theologian or missionary on religious pluralism: "We know what the truth is, and if some other group says something different then that other group must be wrong." We to-day need not give up our view that the sky is not a cow, to find such a position inept. For in this case anyone with any respect for the ancient Egyptians must recognize that they might be wrong, but not simply stupid: not ludicrously wrong, pigheadedly daft. If you know anything of their immensely impressive history, you realize that here were persons not incapable of telling the difference between what you and I call a cow and what you and I call the sky.

Another possible interpretation is that the statement when they made it was not false but meaningless.

Serious, intelligent people, however, whole communities of them, do not, historians can demonstrate, go on making meaningless statements for two thousand years, building great empires in terms of them, producing great art, organizing their corporate and individual lives. We know enough situations when religious statements have in due course *become* meaningless, or less and less meaningful, to considerable groups of persons; and the religious systems of which they are a part then disintegrate or are replaced by new ones. There is a fairly readily discernible difference between a social situation in which the religious beliefs of the group are meaningful to that group, and one in which they are not. In fact, in the history of Egypt one can trace this happening, as ancient-Egyptian culture gave way to Hellenistic, Christian, and then Islamic. The statement became meaningless; and gradually it no longer was made. Yet during the long earlier period when it was made, I am quite sure that it meant something, even though I personally do not see what; and I have never taken the trouble to wrestle with it long enough to find out.

I am confident that if I learned ancient Egyptian as a language and worked in Egyptian art and ideology and all, and studied the matter for a few years, I could find out—and could make it intelligible to you to your satisfaction.

The fact is that you and I would not say that the sky is a cow; and if we did say it, we should be either wrong or absurd. From this it does not follow that for the ancient Egyptians to say it was wrong or absurd. On the contrary: precisely from this it follows that we must listen doubly hard to what it was that they were proclaiming. Because we would not say it, we can realize that differing presuppositions from ours were at work, differing perceptions of the world. Because we would not say it, we can recognize that something was going on here that we are challenged to understand.

Actually, when I say that I do not understand the phrase, I do not mean that I am baffled by it. I mean that I do not have a responsible scholarly, scientific (in the humane sense of the word "scientific") understanding. I have some ideas as to what it might well mean, and to a limited degree believe that I see part (but certainly not all) of what it actually did mean. But I do not know. I am not sure. Such hypotheses as I have framed on the matter I have not confirmed, by extrapolating on the basis of them from contexts that I have studied to new and unrelated ones, so as to verify or to correct my notions: part of the scholar's usual method of procedure. What I think that I discern in this affirmation I do not go on to be able to see as consonant with, supplementary to, coherent with, mutually illuminating of, other affirmations of theirs about the world in which they lived and their relations to it and to their neighbours in it. Nevertheless I do have some hunches as to potential meaning—hunches developed from the Sapir-Whorf interpretations of language,[10] on one hand, and from observations on modern communities living in more I-Thou relationships[11] to the natural environment than we modern Westerners usually do, on another; as well as from the little reading that I have done on this particular matter in Egyptology,[12] and in potentially related fields such as modern Nilotic anthropology,[13] and by hearing about potentially analogous ones such as imagery of sky as cow among Tibetan Buddhists.[14]

If my hunch be correct, and their calling the sky a cow signified among other things that their lives were lived in a more harmonious rapport with nature than they would otherwise have been, and their ability to perceive poetically both cattle and sky was greater, and their sense of corporate life together was enhanced and humanized by sharing symbols in community—if, as I suspect, such matters as these flowed from or were otherwise involved in what they meant when they affirmed that thesis, then I personally would be less ready than are some to judge that they were wrong in affirming it. I would be less ready to pronounce the statement not true.

By "true" I mean, here, having what modern linguistic philosophers would call cognitive value, and not merely emotive or the like, to use the classification that they have ingeniously devised in order to maintain their unfortunate severance of the human and the objective. I am seriously suggesting that the ancient Egyptians' apprehension of their environment evidenced in and made possible through such statements may well have been—however partially or poetically—of a reality that is indeed there. My guess is that they perceived something about the sky, about animals, about themselves, and about the relations among these, that Ayer and his friends have missed. Obtuseness to the Egyptians' insight is not a sure sign of having come closer to the truth about our world.

Is the sky a cow? It would not be true if I said it; but from this it does not follow that it was not at least partially true when they did.

II

This last remark brings us to the historical dimension of our theme; and from the religious we move on next to it as our second heading. The truth may not change; but our approximate apprehensions of it evidently do, and even more conspicuously do the verbal patterns in which we express these to each other. Transitionally to our consideration then of this historical matter, let me recall that the Egyptian example I chose was explicitly tentative. In the case of Islamic, Hindu, and some Buddhist instances we could be much less reticent, less speculative. Many sentences from those systems would appear to critical linguistic analysts as incoherent; one may readily imagine their demonstrating this to their own and their friends' satisfaction. To do so, however, is dishearteningly out of date, surely. To any serious modern student it demonstrates, rather, only that the sentences have not been understood.

For some years I have taught courses and conducted seminars, first at McGill University and later at Harvard, on mediaeval Islamic theology. The analytic philosopher Nielsen, if he were teaching such a course, would have as his purpose, presumably, to persuade his students that they "ought not"[15] to subscribe to its theses, for these are "senseless" and "self-contradictory".[16] (This is pretty much what a hundred years ago some Christians would have aimed at.) A certain type of modern Muslim apologist, if he were teaching it, would presumably have as his goal the persuading of the students that they *should* accept. A certain type of historian would aim at presenting it as illustrative of the Muslim middle ages, its theses to be understood as circumscribed within a closed system now finished and gone. For a humane historian, however, and ideally any historian of religion, such a course of study would be illustrative, certainly, of a given time and place in human history, but not only that. Its being *human* history, and a fortiori these being theological expressions, mean that the system was, and is, not closed. The material is partially anchored in a particular cultural milieu, and is therefore difficult of access to those of us from another; yet is partially open to others of us who also are human, and is illustrative of its authors' having, within and through this particular milieu, been partially open to that transcendence in which all persons variously participate. If one is concerned neither to attack nor to defend these beliefs, but to penetrate and to elucidate them, it turns out that one can come not only to understand them, to learn about them, but also to learn from them. They speak about a universe in which those who composed them, and we who study them, are both involved, however diversely.

Approximately a third or so of the students in such courses have been Muslim, a third Christian, a third other, chiefly skeptics. This has been good, since we have learned from each other, as well as from our texts. (Those not open to such learning excluded themselves, by not joining the courses.) Mediaeval Islamic theology, and the same is demonstrably true of Hindu and Buddhist and of course Jewish thought, has "cognitive value". It has this in that through its perceptive study one comes to know more about human history (an important part of reality), but also about the human condition, about one's fellow human beings, about oneself, and about environing reality.

If every sentence that one meets is imagined to be simply in itself either true or false, then an outsider is easily manoeuvred into not seeing the statements of alien systems as true. If, on the other hand, every sentence is discerned as personal (not excluding in the community sense), as a clue to some person's or persons' vision of reality, then it is much easier to see it as potentially true at least partially, as approximating to truth less or more closely; and indeed as probably true, approximating significantly closely, if millions of intelligent people have found it so. One then settles down to wrestling with that possibility.

I have a hunch that the ancient Egyptians' vision of the world contained some truth, although I do not know. In the case of Islamic, Hindu, and Buddhist visions, let alone Jewish and Christian, I do know.

The difference is not simply that in these latter cases we have moved one or two millenia closer to our own time; but rather that they come from an era of human history that I personally happen to have studied more closely. The ability to understand human discourse is the ability to understand the persons, the community, whose it is. For other ages this is the historian's task. Yet our age too participates in movement.

All language is personal; all persons, communities, are historical. We turn next, then, to consider this latter dimension; not only for others, but also for ourselves.

A philosophy of religion, if it is to be a philosophy of religious language, is hobbled until it recognizes that such language—but indeed all language, including one's own—is human also in this, that it is involved in the dynamism of all human contexts. (Neither this fact of involvement, nor the recognition of this fact, is a limitation. On the contrary!) Meaning and propositional truth, like everything else pertaining to man, are historical; and are to be understood historically. We shall develop this here only in part, since our next chapter will be wholly devoted to one particular illustration of historical change: of how decisive, but also how tricky, it can be in its relation to belief—and our final chapter, to an indication of how, for instance, the reading of scripture is transformed by taking this seriously. For the moment, I content myself with preliminary generalizations, setting forth considerations that are common-place to the historian of religion, but whose absence in others' discussions of these issues can be disconcerting.

The basic point is that everything is in process. Therefore, of any given statement we would ask, not: What does it mean, inherently, statically, absolutely; but rather: What has it meant. What has been its meaning in this or that century; in this or that part of the world; to this or that community? What does it mean to-day, to this group and to that? And eventually, perhaps, but only eventually: What does it, may it, shall it, mean to me?

Since religious symbols, forms, and doctrines tend to be exceptionally perdurable, this particular matter is, paradoxically, both liable to be overlooked, and exceptionally important. The historian is disquieted when it gets overlooked, by either proponents or critics. In the debate that we are considering, both hostile and defensive philosophers seem sometimes to act as if a sentence were true or false, meaningful or meaningless, having this or that significance, in some timeless fashion. If one concentrates, however, for any statement primarily on understanding it, rather than on adjudicating whether it be abstractly true or false, mighty or vacuous, then the time factor (also: the place factor, the group factor) becomes not merely inescapable but illuminating.

Everyone knows (although not everyone notes) that the meaning of words has a history; but so does the meaning of sentences, of languages, of systems of thought. I have been doing some detailed work recently on specific interpretations of 'faith' in Islamic theology. In the course of it I came to feel that two of the

Arabic words in one of the formulae that became established in major groups can be shown to be potentially ambiguous; and I have written articles presenting evidence to Arabist circles to argue that the original meaning, in the chief textual passages that are relevant, was different from what recent Western scholarship has on the whole interpreted it as being. I have gone on, however, to discover and in those articles to elucidate that there has been a discernible history and evolution of the meanings also within the Muslim community. The formula has been read differently by differing groups in different centuries. It is not only the original meaning that is significant but the continuing development of that meaning from era to era, from class to class, from milieu to milieu.

Similarly for so central a matter as scripture. A major step was taken about a century ago in the West in the mounting of a great movement of historical criticism of scripture, both Christian and other, reconstructing the original meaning of each word or context of the Bible, the Bhagavad Gita, the Qur'an, and so on. A second equally major step is only now in process of being taken, in recognizing that the true meaning of any scripture—and by that I mean the empirically real, objectively valid, historically given meaning—is a long, and an on-going, process of which the original meaning is only the starting point, and which is constituted by what the scripture has in fact meant to various persons, groups, movements, over the centuries since: a process that still proceeds. The second step is as revolutionary as the first. To take it is for certain groups as difficult, even intellectually painful, as was the first. It is especially difficult, of course, for what I may call fundamentalists: those whose notion of truth and meaning has jelled, is non-historical. (Nowadays, perhaps, there are at least as many of these among analytic philosophers as there are among religious groups?)

All this is perhaps more obvious for scriptural texts than for doctrines; but not more significant. Once one has learned to see the meanings of either as in unending transition, one finds dull any discussions that leave this out of account. The notion that any statement whatever is, or in principle can be, true or false in itself, meaning this or that inherently: such a notion, I submit, it is helpful to recognize as out-of-date.

What a statement means is what it means to some person or persons, at some time or place. And this varies: if not from person to person, at least from group to group, and from era to era.

The historian of religion finds no religious statement meaningless—especially, none that has been made by serious, intelligent persons, and cherished by substantial groups over considerable periods of time. As we saw in the case of ancient Egypt, and as is true more generally, one may study those occasions when societies have moved away from giving to, and receiving from, such statements a certain meaning or a certain sequence of meanings; and it is the historian's business then to observe and to make observable what is happening. A group's religious beliefs' gradually becoming no longer meaningful is a highly significant process in any society, important to be discerned and understood. Religious meaninglessness, if ever it exists, is a predicate not of statements but of particular persons; and of aberrant social situations, whose development in time can be traced.

Such situations are historically and humanly revealing, certainly: no historical situation but is illuminating of the human condition. Yet it is substantially less interesting, and instructive, to explore these, than to strive to understand rather those—a good deal more common, happily—that constitute the historian's primary focus of attention, and indeed constitute by far the major portion of the history of humankind on this planet: namely, those eras and communities for which religious beliefs, in one or other of a vast variety of sorts, have been not merely meaningful, but indeed more meaningful than any others. It would hardly be unfair to report as an empirical observation that in their religious statements more men and women have invested, and from them have drawn, more meaning, at more times, in more places, than in and from any other kind. The history of these meanings can be ascertained.

Some philosophers would like to find less, and some theologians more, absolute meaning in these statements than this historical orientation would support. To the former I have sufficiently given my answer: the meaning that the historian finds is real, is solid, is demonstrable. To the theologian my answer is equally positive: the meaning that the historian finds, incorporates more truth than the doctrine does. In theological terms, it is closer to God. Religious truth, and falsity, lie not in any statement; but potentially in the actual meaning that that statement has or may have to particular persons in particular historical situations. That meaning, being historical, is not priorly given.

Accordingly, it is a mistake (and we shall see in our next chapter, a recent mistake) for preachers or theologians to try to persuade anyone to believe a given doctrine.[17]

It is vastly more important that one understand it. By this nowadays we mean, that one understand what it has meant to persons in the past, and what it might mean to one to-day. Once having understood, then whether one respond or not, or how, is up to oneself—or to oneself and God. That is faith. Belief, on the other hand, is nowadays a distracting anachronism (as we shall explore a little in our next chapter).

No statement, I have suggested, means anything in itself. It means something only to some person or persons (and always something just slightly different, which is why it has a history). Similarly, no statement is meaningless in itself—at least, none that is put forth seriously, sincerely, by any rational human being. Insofar as it is meaningless, it is always meaningless to somebody. The historian is quite ready to believe that Christian religious statements, or Greek metaphysical ones, are meaningless to certain modern philosophers. At one level, this signifies simply that they have not understood them; although at another level it illustrates, further, a rather complex historical development that has recently taken place.[18]

The historian of religion or of culture is quite accustomed to finding the propositions of one group, or century, not understood by members of another. A slightly curious note is added when, in addition, those who do not understand become rather zealous missionaries endeavouring to persuade others not to understand, either. Of curiosities, however, the history of religion is full; is it perhaps better to be amused by this than offended? What actually is happening here is that the missionary zeal is directed, via the attempted undermining or destruction of an alternative world-view, to proselytizing on behalf of one's own. This is historically standard: we have seen it often before. Modern anti-religious linguistic analysts are not only fundamentalists but iconoclasts; and missionary.

As has been the case with other missionaries, however, although they have misunderstood those against whom they preach, their own position is not without substance, were it not sullied by its deprecating of others'. If the religious communities speak of transcendent matters in mundane and time-bound phrases, their modern philosophic critics speak in grand and would-be timeless terms of matters mundane—though major.

The truth to which, in their somewhat uncouth way, the hostile analysts bear witness, is the poignant fact that Christian beliefs have indeed become meaningless to a large number of modern Western persons; and have become false to many.

It is an historical, rather than a cosmic, reality to which these negative thinkers call attention; a reality to the understanding of which their contribution is at best indirect, but to the importance of which no theologian—nor anyone else concerned for our modern plight—but should be alert. The two sides misunderstand each other, each the victim of an undiscerned historicity, and one the victim of an unseemly and damaging aggressiveness, under which the human situation worsens.

III

This brings us to my third and final point, the comparativist issue. Any religious or philosophic position, it has been found, can be understood better when viewed as within the context of the global whole. Once one has learned to view each position so, and to be self-consciously aware that one's own outlook too takes its place within this larger context, then discussions carried on within the old limitations appear narrow. Variety is basic to religious—and to human—life. He or she who would understand religion must understand diversity.

Let us look at India, that locus *par excellence* of religious diversity. In India not only has the variegated quality of man's religious life been drastic, and conspicuous. More: it is gloried in. Hindus, unlike many others, tend to argue not only that religious life is, but that it ought to be, diverse. Hindus are self-consciously, affirmatively, pluralist. The very concept 'Hinduism', suggesting a system, a structured entity, is inept: the Hindu complex is to India what Comparative Religion is to the world.

Yet there is a further point about the religious situation in India, redoubling the significance of that sub-continent for our purposes: namely, the presence there, these past one thousand years, not only of the Hindu but of the Islamic. Now the Islamic movement also has been diverse, as I have argued that the historian finds every human movement to be. The Islamic enterprise has evinced, in the fourteen hundred years of its rich and multi-faceted history thus far, much dynamics, much creativity. It too has been characterized by variety. Nonetheless, in principle it aims at being unified, systematic, holistic. If of all the major religious traditions of the world the Hindu has been inherently and as it were by intention the most complex, the most exuberant, con-trariwise of them all the Islamic has been inherently and by intention the most coherent, the most systematic.

To have, then, these two traditions both in the same country, presents us not only with diversity in its positive, most elaborate sense, in the Hindu case, but also as it were negatively—by juxta-posing pluralism with the world's most sustained negation of pluralism: Islam.

Most Western students of India have tended to be either so secularizing as hardly to understand religion at all, or else so sympathetic to Hindu universalism and relativism as not to under-stand the Islamic outlook. Some few, although these were rare even among Christians, have been sympathetic to the Islamic thrust but then have found difficulty in appreciating Hindu ebulli-ence. The political cataclysm of 1947, with its massive massacres and tumults, showed that Indians themselves could not at that point construct a political framework capable of holding the two orientations together politically; and not many have done so even intellectually. To understand religious diversity in India is no mean challenge!—to those within, and to observers in the West or elsewhere.

Obviously I cannot in a few moments here rise to that challenge. Yet from this problem I would hope to make one point; even though it must obviously be exceedingly over-simplified. To arrive at it, we shall look first at the Hindu complex, then at the Islamic.

About the Hindu congeries of patterns, the over-simplification to be swiftly made is straightforward: Hindu religious life can be understood only through use of a concept like 'symbol'. This notion 'symbol' is helpful, or indeed requisite, not only for understanding the various data of the Hindu realm, but also for understanding the diversity of those data; and for the understanding of the Hindu acquiescence in, and indeed delight in, that diversity. Hindus perceive the world at large, and almost every item within it, from social hierarchy to thuggery, from asceticism and erotic passion to bed bugs, differently from Westerners, and differently from each other; which fact can be explained in the West either on the hypothesis that they are stupid—which is wrong—or on the recognition that things function symbolically for them. To grasp what is going on here, one needs to recognize that, being human, these men and women perceive transcendence symbolized in a vast variety of mundane forms.

Now this notion of symbol, and the way that it has worked itself out both in practice and in theory in Hindu India, and a growing understanding of both its practice and its theory more recently in the West, have contributed greatly to the modern intellectual study of religious life generally, and indeed of human life generally. An enormous step forward was taken when the symbol idea began to be applied to religious patterns universally.

Thus it was an improvement of no mean proportions when Christians, for instance, began to be interpreted by Muslims, for instance, and by other outsiders, including secularists, not as people who had made the mistake of thinking that a human figure, Jesus, was divine, as Islamic orthodoxy had held, but rather as persons for whom a human figure served as a symbol of the divine, or of the transcendent. Indeed, it has been urged that it is in our day an improvement when Christians themselves begin to say and to recognize this about themselves. In fact, almost the entire history of human religious life is greatly illumined once it is interpreted *in toto* as a history of variegated and ever-shifting symbolism.

I say "almost" the whole of human religious history; but not quite the whole of it. I say that it was an improvement, yet it is still not quite good enough. To return to India: the symbol idea illuminates the Islamic complex; but it does not quite explain it. It is better (more accurate; closer to the truth) to see the Qur'an as a symbol of the divine in the lives of Muslims, from the seventh to the twentieth centuries, and from Spain to China, than to see it as a purely mundane seventh-century Arabian book, written by Muhammad, as Western scholarship used to do, and to insist on doing. How the Qur'an once came to be what it is, can be explained by that traditional scholarship; but how it came to do what it has since done, in the centuries after it came to be, and in country after country also outside Arabia, cannot. To interpret symbolically its subsequent empirical role, stupendously creative, is a major advance. Yet the fact is that it has functioned in the lives of Muslims as something more. In historical actuality, they have regarded it not as a symbol of God, but as quite literally the word of God. Similarly Christians have regarded Christ as divine; not as a symbol of the divine. And for non-theists there is the question: What is the divine a symbol of?

Religion scholarship, then, has accomplished a great deal in appropriating and universalizing the concept 'symbol'; and we all cannot but be grateful. The notion has contributed to human understanding, especially of Indian but also of archaic and of Buddhist and of much other religious experience; and has contributed to self-understanding. Yet it does not quite serve to explain the Islamic. To understand India (and, I would argue, to understand man), one has to understand *both* symbolism and iconoclasm.

No doubt there are in the Islamic instance particular items that serve as atomistic symbols of transcendence, as there are in the Buddhist and Hindu cases, although much more restrainedly, sparsely. Nonetheless, the primary Islamic mood is one of turning away from particular representations, to subsume all phenomena in and under a total coherence, itself transcendent. The Muslims' aniconic thrust has to be reckoned with: their enormous achievement of system, their emphasis on what they call *tawhid*—unity, unification, integration. That Arabic word is usually translated "monotheism", but it means "getting it all together", to use the modern jargon. And the fact is that for several centuries for many hundreds of millions of persons Islam has got it all together remarkably well.

I have observed over the years how easy it is for outsiders to fail to understand Islam; to misapprehend both the total structure on the one hand and (therefore?) the various items within it that are given meaning by it. The problem here is the difficulty of coming to terms with a coherent total system that one does not oneself share; a difficulty that arises in considerable part from looking *at* what those who are concerned with it do not look at, but look through.

What one is wrestling with here is the fact that in the Islamic case it is the total system of Islamic thought that functions, as it were, symbolically. Here we have an integrated world-view, which is very precious to the Muslim group, and which serves them as a pattern for ordering the data of observation, not as among the data to be ordered. It constitutes a conceptual framework within which the universe is framed; the universe and man, life, oneself, one's hopes and failures, frustrations and joys, one's marriage, one's child's illness, all that one sees and knows, says and does. It is not part of what a person knows, but the vision by which he knows, and within which. We may say that within it he knows, or guesses, or is aware of not knowing: even ignorance, even rejection, are inside the system.

The system does not "mean" something, so much as it confers meaning. It is in light of the total system that every word, every proposition, made within it has whatever meaning it has. And not only propositions, but things. Islam is not an item in the pattern of a Muslim's life. Rather, it is the name of that pattern into which all the items of his life cohere. If a Muslim loses his faith, nothing in his life may change; except that the various elements in it no longer cohere into a pattern, are no longer meaningful. Islam is that total framework by being embedded in which each component part of the lives of Muslims, each thing that they see, each object that they touch, each sentence that they utter or receive, takes on meaning.

Within the whole there are certain concepts, such as the concept of God, and certain propositions, such as that the Qur'an is the word of God, that in a subtle fashion derive their meaning from the total Weltanschauung, and also in turn give meaning to that

Weltanschauung. The concept 'God' is the keystone of the whole pattern, no doubt; but is not its totality—and is in the end significant not in isolation, but within the whole. Although analytic philosophers have not paid much attention to systems of thought outside the Western, yet we may readily imagine one of them saying that these concepts and propositions are themselves meaningless. My interpretation of what he is saying here would be simple: that on these propositions meaning is not conferred by or within the Weltanschauung by which *he* sees the world.

In order to understand such statements, as it is my task as an academic historian to do, one must ascertain not what they mean in themselves (I hold that no proposition has meaning in itself), but what they mean (and have meant) within the system within which they are used. One may even go on then to inquire whether, within that system, they are true or false. And if the outsider wishes to say that the system as a whole he rejects, or one ought to reject, one runs into the subtle point that it is not fully clear what is involved in rejecting a symbol as "wrong". This is especially problematic when it is a total Weltanschauung that is functioning symbolically. I myself am hesitant to say that the worldview of the analytic philosophers is wrong; though I observe that it is woefully limited and seems ineptly stultifying. (Even the later Wittgenstein is non-historical and non-integrating.)

But to return to India, and to that Islamic world-view:

Dealing with atomistic symbols, though not easy, is easier than this. Most of us can contrive to get ourselves into the position, even if we do not fall into it naturally, where we grasp what is going on when particular objects of the physical world are being seen as the locus or channel of an otherwise amorphous or an otherwise-conceived transcendence; or, shifting from things to propositions, when sentences are both spoken and heard "metaphorically", rather than literally. This is the kind of thing that Hindus are good at, more than are Muslims; Roman Catholics, more than Calvinists; poets, more than analytical philosophers. The next stage in our development is to comprehend the two at once; to understand both the Hindu and the Islamic in India, and thereby both parts of the split personality of our own Western culture.

No one, I would urge, has understood either the Islamic or the Hindu movements who, however well he may have grasped either separately, has not apprehended the contradictions between them. The incompatibility of the two is part of the truth about each. (The historian does not forget that there have been, also, certain ways that each has developed for reaching out towards the other— for instance, in the Sufi and Bhakti movements: ways of appreciating and recognizing each other. These have been secondary; but they also are part of the truth. Persons may understand, and even perhaps sub-systems; even if systems generally do not.)

Our Western world has some distance yet to go before it rises to self-consciousness in this matter of our over-all ideational frameworks. We do not readily understand the Islamic, just as the Muslim does not readily understand the Hindu. A major reason why we cannot yet grapple well with a total system of this type, is that we are ourselves working within a total system of the same general type, though a different system. We are all iconoclast, but also all iconodule, to use the technical terms for both sides of that classical controversy: we would shatter others' symbols or icons that we do not understand, but we slavishly submit, even unwittingly, to our own.

In the Western world, and especially the academic world, we have hardly begun to become critically aware even on the iconoclast side. Just as (and perhaps this is genetically significant for all of us) the Hebrew world-view cannot stomach idolatry, so our science system is anti-mystical, and our logical systems anti-metaphor. More basic: all our systems, religious *and* secular, are anti-alternative-system.

Modern logic has perpetrated the unsubtlety that every meaningful statement is either true or false. (As riposte to this, one might toy with the thesis that rather, every meaningful statement is an over-simplification. This, one might not wish to defend relentlessly; it would be easy, however, and important, to contend that this aphorism is itself less of an over-simplification than is the black-and-white dictum of the present-day analysts.)

Modern philosophies, Western liberalism, all our ideologies, whether religious or secular, are ways of looking at the world, and are not themselves symbols, are certainly not interpreted as symbols; although it seems not unhelpful to say that they function in some sense symbolically. Yet neither in the religious realm, as we have said, nor in the philosophico-scientific, is the symbol concept quite adequate.

Some comparativists hold, or are suspected of holding, that it does not matter which of many systems one adopts. I am not that kind of relativist. An historian—for instance, of India—cannot fail to note that, at least so far as life on this earth is concerned, it matters a great deal. The consequences are large, and they ramify. (So far as the Day of Judgement is concerned, the historian further notes that theologians of the various traditions, Islamic, Christian and other, in addition to more obvious stands, have regularly held that what will matter then is not what system one has worked within—an alien question—but rather how one has related within it. We shall return to this in our remaining two chapters.) No; systems do differ among themselves, deeply.

Some modern philosophers tend to hold that that system of thought is best that most satisfactorily explains reality. This is fine so far as it goes, but is unduly limited if by "reality" is meant the reality of the non-human world only. It is unduly limited, besides, in that we have not only to interpret reality but also to live with it; and indeed to live with ourselves, and with each other, within it; also to die within it. Further, while we do not have to aspire, historically we men and women have aspired, to live well: to be fully human. This includes, but transcends, thinking rightly.

One might perhaps toy with a suggestion that a criterion for assessment among systems might be the degree to which any given one facilitates a person's relation to self, to neighbour, and to universe—including, so far as the sheerly ideational level is concerned, the relation of intellectual understanding. Once again, of course, both the comparativist and the historian note variety. Each system differs from the others; but also what is called a single system has itself differed from place to place, from century to century, from village to city—in other matters, and also in its success in promoting persons' good relations at the conceptual and at other levels with themselves, with each other, and with the cosmos.

All this is a very large matter. Absolute relativism is to be rejected, on multiple grounds: it is anhistorical, irrational, un-

Christian, un-Islamic, even un-Hindu; although it would take us too far afield to develop this here. Being an historian I am interested in the movement in our day of each traditional system into, through, and perhaps beyond what one might call a relative relativism—without which each is closer to its limited and now inadequate past than to what we may surely hope to construct as our more comprehensive future. The problem, one might say, is how to be pluralist without being simply relativist. Elsewhere[19] I develop some aspects of this rather mighty matter at greater length. Here I wish to make but two points, both of importance to our present topic.

First, I would submit that analytic philosophy (in all its variety and with all its sub-types) is understood best if seen comparatively as one world-view among others. In particular, it has shown itself in many ways comparable, so far as ideas are concerned, to the ideological frames of the religious systems. Secondly, this being so, I shall suggest that we consider in particular its understanding of, judgement upon, fellow systems. The first of these points considers linguistic philosophy in general, basically as a philosophy of (based on) natural science; the second considers in particular its sub-area, philosophy of (about) religion.

The comparativist notes that some systems have been better at some matters, others at others; the historian notes that this too has fluctuated, in small ways and in large. One of the major developments of recent centuries, clearly, has been a change in the matter of a system's theoretical adequacy to the data of the objective world. In the past, the major world-views on earth—Hindu, Islamic, Christian, for instance—although differing, of course, in many ways, were more or less alike in this, that each was pretty much able to comprehend the world that it knew. The adherents of each had, to some appreciable extent, a coherent, rational, serviceable vision making sense of their own lives in community and, so far as they understood them, of the facts of the natural world in which they lived. The theological orthodoxies of each community were impressive intellectual constructs.

A time has come, however, as we all know vividly, when through natural science and technology none of these ideological patterns is able to do anything like justice to the facts of the objective world as we now expansively know these. The historical result is before us: increasingly around the globe persons have been abandoning, in part or *in toto,* these classical ideologies and replacing them with a vision of the world more attuned to, or directly based upon, modern science. Recent academic philosophies, most recently in their linguistic forms, are more or less orthodox articulations based on this newer vision. Linguistic analysis, for instance, explicitly derives from modern objective natural science its sense not only of what is known, but of what it is to know: of meaning, of truth, of significance.

From this fact it derives its force, its confidence, its validity, its prevalence. The spectacular success of science and its well-earned prestige, its attraction for our most brilliant minds, its practical prowess, its affluence, for long its invulnerability to criticism, its constantly emerging victor in every successive conflict, all went into its triumph, some of which spilled over into the movement of its philosophic ally.

History, however, proceeds; and more recently a phase has begun of a recognition that while objective science has been spectacularly successful in dealing with the natural world, the world of things, and in understanding it, it has been less successful, to put it mildly, in dealing with human affairs. The application of theories and methods and outlooks from the natural sciences to the study and organizing of man and society has contributed much to affluence, something to prediction and manipulation, less to understanding, and least of all to understanding human beings specifically as persons, or to understanding human history.

In other words, as with classical religious Weltanschauungen, a phase of self-assurance ("science is knowledge; we are basically right") is followed by one of at least partial dethronement. As is standard whenever a great system passes its zenith, the awareness that it is waning, and especially that it wanes because it is deficient, is resisted by its adherents. The awareness comes slowly and painfully. Nor are they simply obtuse: their perception of the world in terms of their system inoculates them against perceiving the newer truths. In this case the dogmatic pre-conviction, within the belief system, that science (understood in a particular way) and truth are synonymous, accounts for their inability to recognize that their world-view distorts the truth about man, and even about man's true relation to nature. Increasingly this dogmatic preconception, however, is becoming the only reason for not perceiving this; and increasingly only fundamentalists within the movement are failing to sense the crisis.

Of others in this situation some (the "counter-culture") are turning against science; and some would strive for, or settle for, a complementarity that juxtaposes something from each of at least two world-views. Those of us who aspire to continue to honour science and to preserve or to attain integrity, must wrestle with constructing new ideational patterns, ones that will be continuous with and subsume the old visions now seen to be partial, and transcend them. No easy task! At least we can dedicate ourselves with a resolve not to leave out any of the monumental givens.

One upshot is the recognition that no one group among us should absolutize its own premises, its own channels of interpretation (although some linguistic philosophy still tends to do this). The truth has always transcended any human interpretation of it; never more poignantly than to-day. It would be not only ironic but sad if, just when Christians, Muslims, and others are at long last learning to recognize that they are not simply wrong yet neither are they alone right, not fully right, that no one conceptual system is yet adequate—it would be sad if, at just this point, some scientific or philosophic school should seem to say that it alone knows where meaning and significance lie; that it alone can define truth and falsehood.

My second point is that once one has recognized this type of philosophy, as we must, as one in the series, then its assessment of its fellows takes on a different hue. Its judgement of other groups' religious statements becomes recognizable no longer as the verdict of a competent high court, but—alas—as one more instance in the sorry tale of the failures throughout history of world-views to understand each other.

In mediaeval India, of the Islamic system and the Hindu, each in its own way could interpret the universe; but neither could interpret the other.

More generally, however well or not so well any religious pattern has comprehended its adherents' personal lives and the

world in which they lived, most have scored poorly in comprehending other groups. The Christian record in this matter is
particularly doleful: we Christians have sinned much, in misunderstanding and deprecating other positions. At the present time, with
the growing intermingling of communities and the growing awareness of the comparative issue, it is coming to be felt as a major
weakness if one group's system cannot make room for another's.
It would have been pleasant if at least anything so presumably
rational as a philosophy, and so notably modern as a twentieth-
century one, had a good showing on this matter. Disappointingly,
it is no better than the others, and indeed is back where some of
the others were in pre-modern, pre-liberal, times. Here, in linguistic
analysis—especially, of course, in its hostile forms—seems to be a
movement of thought whose incapacity to accommodate, and
even to understand, alternative movements of thought is explicit,
even stark.

It is important to recognize that this fallacy is not, basically, the
result of some flaw in the argument, some lack of rational coherence. Some Christian thinkers have searched busily for these. The
student of religious history would expect none. Orthodoxies, time
and again, have been vastly impressive structures: comprehensive,
internally consistent, and logically rigorous. It is not the logician
who finds them inadequate, but the comparativist historian.

Thus in recent discussions, the position is on occasion set forth
by some analysts that theism, for instance, is so confused and the
sentences in which "God" appears so incoherent and so incapable
of verifiability or falsifiability that to speak of belief or unbelief,
faith or unfaith, in relation to them is logically impossible.
Atheism is as unintelligible as theism; and so is agnosticism, for
there is nothing to be agnostic about; and so is skepticism, for
there is nothing to suspend judgement on.[20]

Now it is important to recognize the justice and the validity of
this affirmation. Speaking as modern philosophers, those who hold
this are right. Altogether right. It is not merely that their logic is
cogent, their reasoning virtually irrefutable, at a technical level;
but that the conclusion is indeed an integral component of their
systematic vision of the world.

The statement and its rightness are not a proclamation of

victory, however; as they themselves imagine, and as some theologians fear. Rather, the position is an admission of defeat. It proclaims aloud that the world-view of those who think this way is incapable of understanding, let alone of taking seriously, alternative world-views, or the persons who hold them.

More accurately one could perhaps say: it does not wish to understand.

Once again, the Christian historian is saddened by this, since his own community has so recently moved out of just such a stage. The polemical tone of the intellectual assault, the self-confidence in the group's own ideational scheme, the lack of imaginative sympathy or appreciation, are to me startlingly similar in this sort of modern linguistic analysis to, for instance, nineteenth-century Christian missionary writing about Islamic or Hindu theology. I have studied the impact of this on Muslims and on Hindus at that time, and know the wounds, as well as the fallacy. The reasoning was vigorous, and those missionaries proved to their own satisfaction and that of their own community that Islamic and Hindu ideas were silly. The historian of religion has sorrowfully to acknowledge that a salient characteristic of religious language has throughout been its ready lending of itself to being misunderstood outside the community of its immediate use. He is also burdened with the recognition of the zealous propensity of those outsiders to misunderstand; and in our day is sobered to find philosophers too joining that company of those who stand on the outside, misconceive, and disparage.

Any system of thought, ostensibly "scientific" or whatever, that finds Christian (or Islamic, or Buddhist) discourse either meaningless or simply false, is announcing that it can understand and interpret the world of physical nature but not the world of man. It is in the same sort of position as would be a scientific theory that could understand and interpret natural phenomena occurring in one sector of the universe only but found itself impotent before observed facts in another. The challenge from philosophers of this school to Christian thinkers to translate what they mean, what their heritage has meant, into the language of this school, and the at times indifferent success of those who have attempted this, may signify nothing more than that that language is indeed incompetent to handle these observed facts. The sector of reality that the historian observes, the reality of human life on this planet, is a good deal too solid and significant for us to be satisfied with a conceptual outlook that cannot do it justice.

Quite apart from the question as to whether linguistic philosophers' understanding of the natural world is fully right, or solely right, there would seem no question but that their understanding of their fellow men is faulty. Therefore, so also is their understanding of themselves.

The appropriate response to exponents of such an outlook is not to pick holes in their argument, although this has at times been bravely done, so much as to recognize and to make patent the poverty and irrationality of their premises. It is the premises of other world-views that they demonstrate to be incompatible with the conclusions of their own. Of the presuppositions of their own, as has been standard also with other outlooks in their heyday, they are, of course, not critical, nor even much aware. The challenge to the rest of us is to elucidate what it is that they take for granted, and to ask what in this they have incorporated gratuitously or omitted irresponsibly—not in order to refute, but in the hopes that both they and the rest of us may move towards positions less inadequate, less limited.

The comparative historian of religion, but for that matter also the devout and pious Christian, note that Christian theology is having to revise itself, however painfully, and as yet however partially, in order to come to terms with the fact that its inherited version of a verbalized view of the world has been but one among several human views, and is one whose validity and serviceability will now limp until it has developed a capacity to do justice to its neighbours' visions—*our* neighbours' visions (as well as to the scientific vision of the natural world). If theology is, as it is often said to be, the conceptualized articulation of faith, then the next great step in theology for us Christians will be the elucidation of a theoretical position that will do justice to our faith, and also to the world in which we hold it, and also to those other communities of faith around the globe in solidarity with whose members we hold it and to respect for whom, and community with whom, our faith itself impels us. Such a theology will be responsive to the religious quality of our development, and to the comparative quality of our modern situation and awareness.

Such a revision is, I feel confident, coming. I myself dream of participating in some small way in its engendering. Something similar holds true for analytic philosophy of religion. It will be painful, I should guess, for it to make the requisite adjustments; and probably these will be slow in coming. Surely, however, it is in principle capable of this development. It would certainly be uncharitable for us to imagine that its proponents are permanently locked within a system unable to adjust to the modern age, unable to cope with the new knowledge that the world history of ideas and the comparative study of culture have made available; permanent victims of a narrow and rigid framework. Like the rest of us, they are surely capable of making the transition from consciousness to critical self-consciousness.

Yet it will not be easy.

I wonder if I am right in speculating that it is from human history, studied comparatively and with sensitivity to its specifically religious quality, that some illumination may come by which we may all move forward.

II. The Modern History of "Believing"

The Drift Away from Faith

MODERN THEORISTS, we have suggested, have tended to misconstrue religious language, and in particular propositional belief. Yet their doing so has occurred within an historical context, the force of which goes far towards explaining, even if not in the end justifying, the narrowness of their vision. They are best understood as having been caught within a great movement of recent Western culture, one that has turned attention in particular directions, has moulded presuppositions, has coloured and almost dictated perceptions, and among other things has changed the meanings of words. It is this last, as illustrative of the whole, at which we shall look in terms of one particular instance in this present chapter.

The development of Western civilization over the past few centuries has of course profoundly affected the human spirit within it, for good and ill; and most participants have shared in the achievements but also in the limitations of its peculiar but powerful outlook. This is so, even though some Westerners have more than others retained from earlier eras certain insights and capacities to which a strictly modern way of seeing and feeling the world would be insensitive; and youth is beginning to go outside the modern West or its currently established culture to recapture these. On the whole, however, critical analysts in philosophy are representative of dominant and almost inescapable trends. In their giving pride of place in religious life to belief, for example, and in belief to statements articulating it in words, they have been aided and abetted, however unwittingly, even by theologians. For a goodly number of Christian thinkers have shown themselves also victims of these same trends. Although differing in their evaluation and interpretation, these thinkers seem to have encouraged, or at least acquiesced in, their critics' locating and formulating of the religious problem.

We shall suggest—elsewhere we argue at length—that those who make belief central to religious life have taken a wrong turning. Our chief task here, however, is to make clear how this error has come about. Anything so firmly rooted in modern consciousness, for both detractors and defenders, cannot be gainsaid or even much discussed short of elucidating the preconceptions out of which it grows, and by which it is nourished. If the views of religious persons, in ancient Egypt or mediaeval Christendom or in India, can be grasped aright only by seeing them within an historical and cultural context, so also the views in modern times of anti-religious polemicists and of those that they combat require, if their true import is to be assessed, a critical awareness of our own culture.

It has been asserted that no culture can be aware of its own presuppositions. This is important, yet is becoming less true in our day than was once the case. For the rise of historical awareness, as well as of comparative-culture sophistication, has provided us with potential appreciation of alternative world-views against which we can then critically apprehend our own. Nonetheless, the assertion has a force and validity that we do well to keep firmly in mind. It is extremely difficult to transcend the culture and the age in which one lives, to any but a minor degree. Even in studying other cultures and other ages, the impulse to order their new data under the rubrics and categories of one's own, to interpret them in terms of one's prior preconceptions, is strong. It is a true feat of rationality, of disciplined imagination, of self-criticism, of creative realism, and of a certain humility, to apprehend intellectually a different outlook; and even more, one's own. Yet one can try.

In the present chapter we shall try this in relation to only one word, and at the historical—not the comparative—level. Yet that one word is so important in modern thought (especially about religion, but not only so); it involves, and has involved, so wide a range of concerns; it has developed meanings so closely intertwined with the basic predispositions of modern Western thought; that it is hard to rise to an awareness of its history. So "natural" does it seem that this word should mean what it means to us, what under the evolution of recent Western culture it has come to mean, that one does not readily imagine a radically different state of affairs, and therefore does not easily recognize what one is doing in thinking thus.

Indeed, one does not easily recognize that in thinking thus one is *doing* anything, in active construction, rather than, passively, merely seeing things in their self-evident state. One resists a recognition that what one of our basic terms has come to mean, far from being inevitable as has been taken for granted, may rather be part of our modern problem.

We shall not truly understand either the "yes" or the "no" answers to our questions, let alone both, until we become aware that the questions themselves are framed in terms that are—have come to be—problematic.

Our word is "belief". Questions currently asked with it include, Are religious (or: Christian) beliefs meaningful or true. My endeavour here is not to answer these questions so much as to discover how both the "yes" and the "no" answers to them have arisen in modern society. I would suggest that the implications of the questions are novel, and on the whole are a distraction from what persons of faith have been centrally involved with, and classically interested in. My hope is to propose more solid ways of coming to terms with religious meaning and religious truth, including Christian meaning and Christian truth.

Meaning and truth are of monumental importance. I by no means wish to set them aside, but rather to engage with them more profoundly and more actively. My contention is that to do so involves looking in another direction from that to which the word "belief" has come in our time to point. Those primarily concerned with beliefs, pro or con, may turn out to be barking up a wrong tree.

Central significance lies, I suggest, with another tree, in a different part of the forest. In my judgement, the primary religious category, and the final human category, is other; is what I call faith; is not belief. This judgement, to which I have slowly come, is based on observation of the religious history of humankind. It is based also on my own personal commitment as an intellectual to the pursuit of rational truth. It has involved as well my personal experience as a Christian living the life of faith. All three components are important, in ways that it would take us too far afield to develop here.

On the first, the comparative religious history of the world, I began my studies long since supposing like any modern Westerner that belief was a basic religious category; that believing was what religious people primarily do. It gradually emerged that this is not so: that an adequate understanding requires attention rather to the different matter of faith. How different, it became important to discern; and what faith is, important to elucidate. For several years I have been preparing a sizeable study,[1] now soon to be published, exploring Buddhist, Islamic, Hindu, mediaeval Christian (specifically *credo*), and Jewish instances of this issue, and constituting perhaps a first step towards constructing a generic conception of faith. The work is an attempt to clarify, in global perspective, the relation between faith and belief; and in particular, to study the former as a major worldwide category, and as significantly different from the latter. For example, it sets forth the point that the concept 'belief' does not occur in the Qur'an. (Similarly, in our next chapter here we shall argue, equally boldly, that it does not occur in the Bible.)

Our present task is more modest—though crucial: namely, to explore how it is that believing, a peripheral notion in world religious history, including Christian, has come in recent Western life to be reckoned so central.

Some years ago I held that the role of belief in Christian as distinct from other forms of the world's religious life had been unusually salient, because of the impact of Greek thought on the Church. The point is, of course, not negligible. Yet it was formulated before I had discovered how recent, and how aberrational, even in Christian thought are modern belief emphases. I argued[2] that faith finds expression in many forms: ritualist, artistic, moral, communal, personal character, and many others, including conceptual—with intellectual expressions of faith, in doctrine, being particularly characteristic of Christians. I still hold this so; but have discovered that this predilection of the Christian Church has been manoeuvred by modern conditions into strikingly novel forms. The issue as modernity has inherited it is much more recent, and also more tricky, than was previously recognized.

Especially, I have found that what it means to believe anything, and especially anything religious, has changed strikingly in recent times. It is this point that I wish to develop here. The theological, and the philosophic, implications of this discovery seem to me large; but these we shall not here pursue.

Some philosophers and others, especially outsiders, appear to feel in our day that faith is belief; most theologians would hold that it is more than belief; I, that it is other than belief. More accurately, I observe that belief has historically become other.

Not only have Christians believed differently from Muslims, and both from Buddhists, as everyone knows (although whether and how their *faith* has been diverse or similar is less easy to say). Not only have Christians of one century believed differently from those of another (although again, whether true continuity has been or should be in faith, despite shifts in belief, is an important question). Not only has the role of believing, in its relation to faith, varied greatly: from century to century, and from group to group. In addition to all this, it can be demonstrated that the very notion of believing has itself been changing, drastically. Specifically in our case, the English word "believe" has, in usage, connotation, and denotation, undergone an arresting transformation. The change seems to have taken place unnoticed, so that a major new development in religious history has happened, as it were, casually.

The shift has been a transition from a concern with something else to a concern with belief. The process has been evinced in the form of a massive shift in meaning of a word; and can be raised into consciousness if we can reconstruct and reckon with the history of that shift. The word "believing" has persisted; but its meaning and usage have changed.

We have grown accustomed to recognizing that other peoples and other eras have believed differently from us. Less vivid is our realizing that they have meant something different by "believing". In our first chapter, I argued that of any given statement one should ask what it has meant to particular persons. In this present one, I suggest that this historical and personalist principle is applicable also to believing as such. One should ask: What has it meant to believe. What has it been meaning, to various people, religious and secular; various groups; various centuries?

We shall here attempt to answer this for the English-speaking world from early modern times.

I

To begin the investigation, one should first glance at the mediaeval background; but that is primarily a matter of, rather, faith, and is examined therefore at length in my other study. Here we content ourselves with a few hasty observations only. So far as Latin is concerned, the word for belief is *opinio*. "To believe" is *opinor, opinari*. These constituted an almost negligible category in mediaeval Christian thought. No one imagined that faith was this; and the relation between faith and this was not canvassed. As we shall see in our next chapter with regard to the Bible, belief was not a religious category. In my other study I argue[3] that it is an anachronism, and given the intervening developments has become a mistranslation, to render *credit* as "he believes". *Credo* literally means "I set my heart" (from *cor, cordis*, heart, as in "cordial", "concord", and the cognate "electrocardiogram"; and **-do, *-dere*, to put[4]). In St. Thomas Aquinas, for instance, and indeed as late as Vatican I, this verb means to pledge allegiance, to commit oneself, to give one's loyalty. So far as its purely conceptualist aspect is concerned, which for some thinkers loomed larger than for others, it signified not "to believe" but "to recognize", as we shall consider in our next chapter. Far from faith's being interpreted as a matter of belief, throughout the Middle Ages *vice versa: credo* was, rather, squarely a matter of that "something else" that the Church perceived as "faith".

That "something else" I continue to call faith; some moderns, admittedly, have subjected that word also to the same shift so that it too means for them more or less what "belief" has come to mean. What it classically meant, and what it should or shall generically mean, I leave to my other study.

Turning from Latin to Mediaeval English, there is no question but that the Anglo-Saxon-derived word "believe" in its various forms meant in earlier centuries pretty much what its exact counterpart in German, *belieben,* still means today: namely, "to hold dear", "to prize". It signified to love (it comes from the same root as "love": German *Liebe,* Latin *libido*), to give allegiance, to be loyal to; to value highly. Of this early usage, I set forth considerable materials illustratively elsewhere,[5] and accordingly here

merely remark in passing on such facts as that the several manuscripts of a same mediaeval work may read "leve", "love", "beleue" as virtually equivalent variants;[6] and that, in Chaucer's
Canterbury Tales, the words "accepte my bileve"[7] mean, simply:
Accept my loyalty; receive me as one who submits himself to you.
This was the term chosen to serve as the action word designating
the movement by which a person gave his heart to his heavenly
Lord, entering—deliberately, through an act of will—into a relationship of personal allegiance. Thus it can be shown that the
phrase "belief in God" originally meant in English a loyal pledging
of oneself to God, a decision and commitment to live one's life in
His service.

Now the difficulty of our task—the heavy demand made upon
us to apprehend what was actually going on here—derives from the
fact that we tend to be impelled to read this phrase's modern
meaning into this ancient wording: not instead of its then meaning, once we are alert; but in addition to it, unless we are quite
exceptionally alert. For is it not of course the case that this way of
verbalizing this act—as "belief in God"—presupposes God's existence; so that it is extraordinarily taxing for a modern not to hold
that a mediaeval who "believed in God" in the sense of actively
giving Him his allegiance was also and therein believing in Him in
to-day's sense of opining that He is? No doubt the conceptual
framework was there; but not "also", and not "therein", and not
"in to-day's sense".

We shall return to this presently, in our brief discussion of the
emergence in the twentieth century of a use of "believe" in the
sense of presupposing: and I explore it at greater length in relation
to the Islamic complex in the larger historical-comparative study
to which I have referred[8]—these matters being often seen more
clearly if one look outside one's own culture. Suffice it here to
suggest two small points only as potential illuminators for us of
the situation.

First, it is true that the mediaeval who said, I formally pledge
my allegiance to God (*credo in Deum*, "I believe—bilieve, beleeve,
etc.—in God") participated as did his fellows in an intellectual
world-view that included the concept 'God'. Yet it is no less and
no more true that the mediaeval who said, I renounce the Devil,

participated in one that included the concept 'Devil'. Nonetheless, in the latter case we have but little difficulty in discriminating between his renouncing and his believing / presupposing. The word "renounce" does not, and never did, mean "believe", even though no one did or does renounce anything without believing.

Secondly, the performative "I do" in the traditional marriage service no doubt may be seen as implying that the speaker, and indeed all the company, accept, and even in some fashion by the very assertion re-affirm, marriage as a given institution. Yet although in the assertion this is presupposed, it is not what the assertion asserts. It is certainly not what, oriented rather to a specific person as marriage partner, it primarily means. A libertine who does not believe in marriage might argue that a friend's "I do" is meaningless; but he would be wrong. Much is presupposed in, everything that we say; and there might perhaps be merit in coming to recognize that included somewhere in the meaning of every particular word and sentence is the entire Weltanschauung within which in its particular and limited way it is meaningful. There is no merit, however, in performing this act of sophistication solely for the erstwhile word "believe", thereby misunderstanding it.

The marriage analogy has the interesting added advantage, however, of suggesting an historical dimension. For whereas in earlier centuries the element of postulating or affirming marriage as an institution, in addition to taking the vow of fidelity to a particular partner, within the accepted ideological and social system, was minimal (and at a conscious level, perhaps zero), so utterly taken for granted was that system in the community and in the minds of its members, yet nowadays in the late twentieth century when that system is seen as less prevailing, is less automatically presupposed, the allegiance that the bride and groom swear to each other is perhaps beginning to be also an expression of allegiance to the system as such. A time may come when this will grow?

Similarly, with a performative such as "I promise . . . ", which presupposes tacitly a recognition of moral obligations generally and of the sanctity of promising, in addition to expressing the specific undertaking.

To return to the history of religion. Through many Christian centuries the ceremonial *credo* by which one joined the Church, or the re-iterated but also ceremonial and activist "I believe" of the Sunday-service creed, was strikingly like the performative "I do" of a marriage service, was a promise, and bore no resemblance to the descriptive propositionalism of a modern theorist's reporting on the current state of his opinions.

Indeed, one might perhaps sum up one aspect of the history of these matters over the past few centuries in the following way. The affirmation "I believe in God" used to mean: "Given the reality of God as a fact of the universe, I hereby pledge to Him my heart and soul. I committedly opt to live in loyalty to Him. I offer my life to be judged by Him, trusting His mercy". To-day the statement may be taken by some as meaning: "Given the uncertainty as to whether there be a God or not, as a fact of modern life, I announce that my opinion is 'yes'. I judge God to be existent". Insofar as a moral commitment and one's life behaviour are involved, they could add: "And I trust my judgement". To say that so-and-so believes in God may mean: The idea of God is part of the furniture of that man's mind.

Only those sensitive to the enormous difference between these two, and aware then of what a radical transformation has taken place in the history of religious thought and life, are in a position to reflect adequately on religious language.

This is, however, as we have indicated, only one aspect of the shift that has been effected. It has been a multi-faceted development. Not only has the transformation occurred, an historian notes; further, it is possible to trace the process of its happening— to see various steps by which it advanced, and various elements of which it was constituted.

We begin with an observation of the Bible and its 1611 rendering into English in the Authorized Version of King James, a not merely illustrative but mightily consequential translation. We have remarked that in the scripture itself the great concept is faith, and that a concept of belief is not found. That matter we shall pursue in our next chapter. Here we note a statistical fact, concerning not concepts but words. In that 1611 English version, the word "faith" occurs 233 times; the word "belief", once.[9]

Immediately, however, a complication arises. The above figures have to do with the nouns. Both in Hebrew and—of more special importance for our purposes—in Greek, there is a verbal form to go along with the noun-concept 'faith'. In English, there is not. Where the scripture sets forth this central Christian notion ('-m-n, pist-) in its verbal mode, the translators rendered it by the English verb "to believe". It is not that they misunderstood their text. Rather, it is because at that time as we have insistently affirmed this verb did indeed signify, not what it has come to mean to-day, but that cognate something else: the "act of faith", as Roman Catholics still call it.

Shakespeare also, we may note, illustrates a comparable situation. In his plays, the figures are: "faith", 452; "belief", 15. The verb "believe", however, is fairly common with him,[10] in usages that we shall discuss presently.

This particular linguistic bifurcation in English underlies part of the diverging development that we shall explore. For one thing, while "faith" has remained a primarily religious term—and its correlatives "faithful" and the like, primarily moral—"believing" and "belief" have become much more secularized. (The subsequent history of the term "faith" has not been uninfluenced by that of its verbal counterpart, of course, but it has evinced substantial independence. We shall not pursue it.)

If one sets out to analyse the changing history of the meaning of believing from early modern times until to-day, at least three major transitions in the usage of the English word can, I have discovered, be observed. They are far from minor. The first two are from the personal to the impersonal. The third is from the true towards the dubious and the false. Let us see these trends in process.

We shall examine a long-range shift, first, in the grammatical object of the verb; second, in the subject of the verb; and third, in the surrounding context of usage. Each is revealing; together, they have been crucial.

As background for all our discussion, I would ask the reader unrelentingly to recall that the word "believe" in English meant primarily to hold dear, to belove, to treasure, and seems to have been popularized in the language primarily as a Christian technical term. The sense of "trust" was also prominent. Let us investigate its later development, under our three headings.

II

First, we observe the shift in the object of the verb. In the Bible, the verb "believe" is used as follows:

With no object	34%
Personal object	41%
Thing as object (including word, promise, etc.)	12%
Propositional object ("that . . ." clause)	12%

These statistics are of basic significance for our problem; and will repay being carefully pondered. The matter of no expressed object had been standard in early usage: it is found for most early entries in the Oxford English Dictionary for the noun "belief", and continues also with later writers, though decreasingly. We shall not pursue it here; it will occupy us in our next chapter's discussion specifically of the Bible. Our present concern is, rather, with the object as person.

Here in the early seventeenth century, in this religious document, the verb "believe" names chiefly a relation to a person. This had become the prevalent usage. Shakespeare also has a direct personal object as his most common usage: "I believe you", "Who will believe us?" and the like. (At this point, we note only the fact of this usage, without yet considering its then meaning.) Similarly, a little later, Francis Bacon. For him the predominant sort of belief is "belief in a man".[11] Writing a generation or more later, Hobbes also, with the verb, writes, "beleeve a man";[12] "to beleeve any Person";[13] "whom . . . we beleeve", "whom . . . [they] beleeved", "the Person whom they beleeved".[14] He once remarks that "I beleeve in" is "never used but in the writings of Divines", others (he avers) saying rather, "I beleeve him; I trust him; I have faith in him; I rely on him"[15]—although he gainsays the former view, only two paragraphs further on, by himself writing of the "person we believe in, or trust in, and whose word we take, the object of our Faith",[16] and elsewhere he himself freely and un-self-consciously writes the phrase "beleeve in him".[17] Apparently his point is that the odd clerical usage of "believing in" to which he refers is curious because it deviates from the pattern that we have noted, it signifying "not", he says, as presumably one would expect, "trust in the Person; but Confession and acknowledgement of the Doctrine".[18] This evidently he finds a little strange. He himself, however, has also moved a certain distance along the road towards propositional belief.

For the second step in this particular process, which Bacon[19] and Hobbes also took, is believing a person's word: either in general, or a specific assertion. These are intermediary, both historically and logically, between esteeming and trusting the person, putting confidence in his character (standard in the sixteenth century), and accepting a verbal statement (beginning to be common in the eighteenth). Prior even to them is the quite tricky matter of not a statement but a promise, in which the component of trust in the person is especially high. The case is somewhat intermediate with a prediction. Modern linguistic philosophers tend to hold that promises are not propositions. In their world-view, promises are not true or false when uttered (and when believed). Nonetheless they are verbal; are believable; and are constituted by a subject-predicate complex. I have not collected data, however, specifically on "belief" having as its object a person's statement in the future tense.

The historical point at which Hobbes is to be located in our development is suggested by his rendering of the phrase "to believe in God". His explication differs from both earlier and later interpretations. He says that it signifies "to hold all for truth they heare him say".[20] That is, to believe in God means to regard Him as veracious.

In similar vein, by Hobbes "belief" is explicitly distinguished from opinion[21] (or: from other kinds of opinion[22]), by its combining faith in a person who speaks with credence of his statement: ". . . Beleefe, both of the man, and of the truth of what he sayes. So that in Beleefe are two opinions; one of the saying of the man; the other of his vertue".[23] He defines belief, accordingly, as the admittance of an opinion "out of trust to other men".[24]

(This personalized and veracity-oriented usage of the word still survives to-day among some Roman Catholics, although it has entirely disappeared long since among Protestants and the general secularized public.)

So far was Hobbes moving in the direction of a situation where "believing" or trusting a person has become an accepting of that person's verbal statement, that at one point he even affirms: "it is impossible to beleeve any Person, before we know what he saith".[25] In modern English, this meaning would still be expressed by the phrase "believing a person"; but not "believing in a person". "To believe a person" has with us come to mean, to accept as true what he is saying, and usually only that; without regard, any longer, to what he does, or feels, or is, or even to trusting him. "I believe his statement, but I do not trust him" is in our century not a contradiction in terms.

Locke, half-a-century later, used the word "faith" for "assent to any proposition . . . upon the credit of the proposer",[26] much as Hobbes before him had done for "belief". Locke defined the word "belief", on the other hand, without reference to that personalizing dimension, characterizing it along with "assent" and "opinion" as "the admitting or receiving any proposition for true, upon arguments or proofs that are found to persuade us . . . without certain knowledge. . . ."[27] In actual practice, however, I find that Locke usually did employ "believe" (as a verb) in connection with a trusting of the proponents.[28] Even with Hume in the eighteenth century, we shall see presently, "belief" is although often yet by no means solely of the propositional type. It is in the nineteenth century that this becomes dominant in non-religious writings.

So generally is our present world heir of these secularist developments in the nineteenth century that we must take careful note of the new positions. By 1843 John Stuart Mill could write: "the simplest act of belief supposes, and has something to do with, *two* objects".[29] What he has in mind is propositional belief, of the type "to believe that . . .", and more specifically, "He believes that A is B". This remark occurs in his book on logic, and is a mistake to which subsequent logicians have been particularly prone. It is only fair to them to recognize, however, that by the nineteenth century, and on into the twentieth, this particular sort of "believing" had indeed become widespread, and has continued to grow. To take a present-day example, John Laird of Aberdeen in an encyclopaedia article on "Belief" writes explicitly: ". . . what we actually believe is always a proposition or set of propositions. Of these, creeds are composed".[30] He goes on to say: "there are no sub-propositional beliefs"—the use of "sub-" here is delightful, suggesting that if there *were* other kinds of belief, they would be of a lower order.

Now as a matter of fact creeds are *not* composed of propositions (even if moderns often read them as if they were). Neither the Apostles' Creed nor the Nicene contains a single proposition.[31] Into that, however, we cannot go here. Not the classical significance of creeds[32] but the recent (mis-?) understanding of what subscribing to them signifies, is our topic.

Into this realm as well as others has infiltrated the innovating idea that the verb "believe" has as its proper complement a double object. In Shakespeare, this verb had been used with one object much more often than with two.[33] As we have already seen, the same is true for Bacon, Hobbes, and Locke; to say nothing of the King James Authorized Version of the English Bible, where double objects constitute one case in eight.

Mill's statement, then, is manifestly anhistorical. Statistically, such evidence as I have collected suggests that it is grossly awry for most centuries until his own, even though already in the eighteenth the movement can no doubt be discerned as strongly under way, outside the Church. In that century among some intellectuals it had begun to move from being a secondary (originally, a tertiary) usage towards its later perhaps primary position. As late as 1888, however, the Oxford English Dictionary defines "belief" as, first, "the mental action, condition, or habit, of trusting to or confiding in a person or thing", and only secondly as "mental acceptance of a proposition, statement or fact as true".[34] Further one may note that in the twentieth century some dictionaries maintain this order (perhaps for chronological reasons) for the two meanings, such as Webster's Third International, and the American Heritage, while a few reverse it, such as Random House, to mention three from this other side of the Atlantic appearing in the 1960's.[35] None of these, however, nor any other English dictionary that I have consulted from the seventeenth century to the present, lists only the propositional.

Mill was therefore wrong in saying, as he did, in another place,

that "the objects of all Belief and of all Inquiry express themselves in propositions".[36]

Nonetheless he was making, certainly, a major point, of large
consequence for our concerns here. He was not merely registering
a tendency of his time, but strengthening it. He was elevating into
prominence a usage of our term that had become substantially
significant; and the force of his considerable intellect and influence was directed towards making it dominant, if not, as he
urged, exclusive.

In the twentieth century, proponents of this movement, and of
the world-view from which it derives and to which in turn it
contributes, are restlessly semi-aware that ordinary language is not
with them on this propositionalist matter. Accordingly, they have
tried vigorously to impose it. Their usual way of formulating the
issue, taken up also by some theologians, has been to distinguish
between "believing in" and "believing that". It is then urged
(sometimes rather dogmatically) that sentences using the former in
effect "ought" to use the latter; or they "reduce" (their term) the
one to the other. This is a very interesting development; we shall
presently consider how an historical perspective can make much
more manageable and straightforward for us what has been for
static philosophic analysis a somewhat teasing issue. In the meantime, we must give due weight to the influence of this one
particular way of perceiving the world, and its attempt to make
others conform.

For persons of this outlook, propositions are basic. And they
would claim that it is possible (and assume that it is good) to
translate other people's perceptions into their kind of language.
Yet they go on in effect to admit failure in this, as we remarked
in our opening chapter; since the translations do not, in fact, come
out very well. Were it not for the historico-cultural determination
which illumines the outlook, it might seem a trifle odd to insist
that all belief modes càn be transformed into propositional statements, and then to aver that in the translated versions they are not
meaningful. Might it not seem preferable to go back to the original
to see what *it* had meant? However that may be, this school has
arrived at the point where the word "belief" is interpreted as
meaning only something to which a proposition constitutes an
appropriate object.

In his recent Gifford Lectures, Ayer extends this even to "faith". "Until we have an intelligible proposition before us, there is nothing for faith to get to work on", he writes.[37] One must assume a certain innocence here; for he surely does not know how preposterous this is. Yet it is a revealing doctrine (it is too ingenuous to be called a dogma). Historically, most men's and women's faith has been in a person, a moral imperative, a transcendent reality (or simply: in reality), or other non-propositions.

Would it be too provocative to say here: non-propositional truths? Egyptians, Buddhists, Hindus, Muslims, Jews, Christians would classically say it; and it is not clear but that philosophers in the twenty-first century will once again discuss those forms of truth. In the late twentieth, however, many cannot; even though the attempt to turn these into propositions has, on their own account as well as ours, not succeeded very well.

For this movement in connection with belief is part of, and therefore consistent with, a larger ideological development, according to which truth itself is seen as primarily, or indeed exclusively, propositional. This has come to be a prevalent presupposition in certain sectors of our culture, as we have remarked, though its novelty is beginning to be recognized, and its pitiable limitations are beginning to be felt. Mill was one of its champions. He it was who wrote, preposterously: "All truth and all error lie in propositions. What, by a convenient misapplication of an abstract term, we call a Truth, is simply a True Proposition; and errors are false propositions".[38] One may find this not merely wrong, but tragically wrong.[39] Yet one must not under-estimate its formidable historical significance.

A history of the concept of truth is, of course, much beyond our scope here. That would require a major study indeed! We return to our particular concern, the conception of believing: it is not at all surprising that, given the force of this general outlook in recent history of Western society, this specific conception too has been affected. It is important to grasp that by "believe" has come to be signified for many nowadays that mental act or state of which a proposition is the prescribed goal.

Here my first point has been simply to document that the conception has come a long way from where it started. I leave aside my second, the suggestion that to understand this development, and to discern its great significance, including theological significance, for the cultural period that is in our day drawing to a close, are central tasks for the historian both of philosophy and of religion, and certainly for any creative humane—let alone, religious—thinking that is to be helpful for the world in its next steps.

The full import of this development towards propositionalism cannot be grasped, however, until we attend to the second major transition to which I would call attention. Not only the object of the verb, but its subject, has undergone in English usage decisive change. We turn now to that.

III

This second shift, though equally serious and deep, has been basically simple. We may start with Shakespeare. "Believe", as we have remarked, is among his more common verbs. We have also noted that in his diction, believing a person is more common than believing a proposition. No less illuminating is that with him the verb is used chiefly in the first person. It is found regularly also in the second person, especially in the personalized imperative, "Believe me"; hardly at all in the third person. "I believe" is to "he believes" and "they believe" combined, in a ratio of roughly nine to one.

Over 90 per cent of the occurrences of the verb in all its forms—active, passive mood; present, past, future tense; participle; etc.—are of the first and second singular; with the first markedly leading.[40]

With other writers, except for the English Bible postponed for discussion to our next chapter, my observations have not taken the form of a systematic, arithmetically thorough, count. I have observed, however, and should be happy if anyone can confirm or modify this, that not only in Bacon, Hobbes, and Locke is the use of the first person (often plural) standard with the verb "believe", but that also as late as the eighteenth century and with as "unbelieving" a writer as Hume this is still fairly common.[41] At the present time, on the other hand, and especially in philosophic discussions, what other people believe has become the chief focus of attention. The word has come to mean primarily something that other people do.

Although my data are not yet sufficient to verify the hypothesis, my evidence strongly suggests that the ratio of "I believe" (also, of "you believe") to "he believes" and "they believe" has been consistently and markedly less for each century from the fifteenth. This is for the written usage. Ordinary language, to use that phrase, would seem to have followed, but more slowly. At the present time, perhaps especially in the United States, a similar decreasing ratio seems to obtain as one moves from colloquial usage ("you better believe",[42] "I don't believe a word of it") on up (should we say: down?) to academic. So far as sophisticated writing is concerned, however, and analytic reflection, the tendency has definitely been away from oneself and one's friends towards the impersonal.

A whole series of changes is involved in this shift.

For one thing, if one is going to consider languages as the locus of meaning, as linguistic philosophers have come to do, then one should note that inescapably "believe" means something subtly but consequentially different in the two forms "he believes" and "I believe". Not only is the latter self-engaging. Further, it involves, even when its object is abstractly propositional, a statement descriptive of the external world. "He believes" is, strictly, descriptive only of the state of his mind. "I believe that it is raining" is a statement about the weather. "He believes that it is raining" is not.[43]

The self-engagement matter is itself important, and has received consideration. The Christian philosopher Donald Evans, for instance, has a book[44] on the logic of it. For our present purposes, probably the important consideration is the inverse one, of drawing attention rather to the peculiar specificity of another logic, such as the one that has come of late to prevail, that deals primarily or even only with third-person or no-person propositions. Curious is not the logic of personal involvement, but the fact that modern society has developed and in general enthroned rather a logic that ignores or evades it. Curious or not, however, historically one must recognize how important its novel outlook has indeed become.

One may note in passing that Kant argued that believing in God is a rational certainty valid only in the first person singular.[45]

Next, we note one further difference concomitant with the prevalence of the third-person form of our word. It has made feasible this verb's use, in recent times (chiefly the twentieth century) in relation to presuppositions, to conceptual frameworks or patterns of categories through which a community or a culture views the world. Every human life is lived, and every human utterance—as I have been at pains to stress—has meaning, only within a given universe of discourse. Of these in their variety human history has been and continues to be the arena of many. (In simpler times, each society had ideally one; in a modern complex society, and perhaps even in most of its individual members, several may co-exist.) For these some choose the German word *Weltanschauung*; some to-day would call them "languages", *à la* Wittgenstein. They have also, however, been denominated "belief systems". A person is said to "believe" an array of theses that together constitute his outlook on the world, however unconscious he may be of these as theses, or of the pattern of these as a complex of ideas at which one may objectively look.

A perceptive student may infer and state the presuppositions of other persons (this is a considerable part of the task of the comparative historian of religion). It may then be said that those persons believe or have believed such-and-such. One does well, however, to recognize as an innovation the sense in which people "believe" an ideational scheme of which they are unconscious. The difference can be quite major between "believing" in this form of tacitly presupposing, and believing in the earlier sense of actively opting to credit something of which one weighs up the pros and cons. One can come to believe anything in the latter sense, and indeed can understand any proposition's meaning, only in terms of some "language" or system or "belief" in the prior, underlying, sense.

One of the entrancing divergences between the two is manifested in that "believe" in the sense of "presuppose" cannot be used in the first person.[46] What is truly taken for granted is not, perhaps cannot be, explicated. An Andaman Islander had no occasion to announce, to himself or to his fellows, that his mind operated within the Andaman Island world-view.

In classical religious life, *credo* and "I believe" were at their boldest and most intense in the first person singular. Clearly the word has come to designate something different when it is used to describe about me what other people can discern more readily than can I.

It is for this reason that I have held over this point for consideration under this present heading. It could also have come under our earlier one of the object of the verb, in whose on-going movement it has come now to constitute a fourth stage, in which that object is an unarticulated complex of tacit ideas, a conceptual system, so that one is thus said to believe one's presuppositions. Thus, in the process of shift the object moves one step still further down, after a person, a thing, a proposition, to what is not yet formulated.

Yet our considering this development now under the subject, rather, of the verb has the special significance of calling attention to what has been of prime importance both logically and religiously; of prime significance historically. For it is the outsider who notices, and calls attention to, beliefs in this sense. And it is for those concerned that the transition is crucial, from presupposition to self-awareness. One can hardly formulate what one takes for granted. More poignantly, one can no longer take for granted what has once been formulated. It can no longer be "pre"-supposed. What was once unconsciously presumed, "believed" in this novel sense, can then be believed only in another, quite different, sense of our term; or perhaps can no longer be believed at all. Into this latter matter we do not here go: whether erstwhile tacit world-views (or any one among them) can be replaced by less innocent versions—usually mediated by outsiders' analyses—objectively articulated and self-consciously chosen. The former matter, rather, we would stress: that whatever be done about the earlier context and pattern of thinking, the doing of it is now in principle and by logical necessity novel.

What a person or group or era tacitly assumes is exceedingly important, I have long contended—the particular presuppositions of the linguistic school of philosophy being a case in point. Nonetheless, to apply the verb "believe" to these was an innovation; and it modifies the meaning of the verb radically. One hardly does well not to grasp the divergence, and certainly the lack of transferability, between this conception of what other people unwittingly do (or in the past did), on the one hand, and on the other what oneself may now do in self-awareness, or shall in the future do as deliberate option.

It is not strictly necessary that preconceptions be unconscious; only that they not be explicit. Of the many novelties that believing as thus presupposing has introduced, here is one. If I say, "I believe that you speak French", this presupposes that I believe that you speak English; otherwise I would not phrase it that way. Yet it is unduly sophisticated to aver that the sentence "I believe that you speak French" actually means "I believe that you speak English". Similarly, if a sixteenth-century Englishman said, "I believe in God", this no doubt implies that he believed, in this twentieth-century sense, that God exists. Yet he did not say that; and it is misleading, I suggest, to aver that he meant it.

A further nuance:

It is possible that if I say to someone "I believe that you speak French", I may be wrong in what I presuppose (namely: that he speaks English) and right in what I affirm (namely: that he speaks French). Whether similarly a religious credal affirmation may be in its presuppositions faulty, or culturally specific, or poetically imaginative, but in its substantive meaning true and universally valid, for the moment I leave, perhaps tantalizingly, aside. (Yet I suggest that if one is interested in Buddhists or Muslims, one not leave it aside very long; and for that matter, if one is interested in mediaeval Christians. As we argued in our opening chapter, to understand what anyone is saying, one must get beyond, not become bogged down in, the conceptual framework in which he is saying it.)

However one may sort out the truth question, the historical fact is that belief in the third person, belief of other people, has come to be seen largely as a question of prior orientation, of ideational pattern, of the framework within which the drama of life, and of faith, has been staged, rather than of that drama itself. Believing designates no longer an act but a state of mind; and indicates no longer a quality of personal life but the terms of reference in relation to which that quality is articulated.

We turn next to another significant fashion in which the meaning of the verb may or must differ, in the form "he believes" from what it signifies in "I believe". This is in its relation to knowledge; and to truth and falsehood. The new *Encyclopaedia Britannica III* (1974) has only a small micro-entry Belief; but the 1973 edition had a substantial one (by H. H. Price) which contains this sentence: "It is never a contradiction to say 'What *A* believes is false,' but it is, of course, a contradiction to say 'What *A* knows is false' ".[47] Not many readers, perhaps, stopped to reflect, nor were they invited to the reflection, that it is a contradiction to say, "What I believe is false". The implications of this point are elaborate; we shall return to it in our next section.

Meanwhile, let us look at a still further development. Not only has the object of the verb moved downwards from person to proposition, and beyond. Not only has the subject moved sideways off to a distance, from first person to third. Furthermore, to this also we must now add, "and beyond". For still more recently, still more impersonally, abstractly, as we began to see in our last chapter the propositional object has come to be wrenched from all personalist involvement, uprooted from its subject altogether, and stared at out of context. It has been remarked that modern philosophers are not at their ease until they have written down a proposition on the blackboard to have a look at it.[48] Their analysis has as its locus that blackboard, where the proposition is examined minus the verb introducing it.

An example we might go back to that matter alluded to, of the ancient Egyptians' perceiving the world around them in such a way as, *inter alia,* to aver the sky a cow. Now the modern theorists do not, in general, write down on the blackboard the statement, "The ancient Egyptians believed that the sky is a cow". Actually, the ancient Egyptians said that the sky is a cow, and so pictured it; as our discussion thus far corroborates, there are several senses of the word "believe" in which I am not sure that they believed it; but we may let that pass. They did proclaim it; and this is an historical fact, sheer, hard, real—a fact before which we as students of the world of man must have the same basic reverence that the natural scientist has before the brute facts of the world of physical nature, which facts if he cannot understand he must keep striving to revise his theories until he does. But no: the standard procedure here is not to write down, "The ancient Egyptians held the sky to be a cow", which is true, and is important. Rather, they write down simply the proposition, "The sky is a cow"—which appears to be an absurdity. Taken by and of itself, it is so analysed.

Before we turn, next, to our third major trend, let us summarize these first two taken together: that is, the growing impersonalism both of the object and of the subject of our verb; and the growing abstraction. "Believe" is a word that used to conceptualize something solid in the realm of interpersonal relations. "The basic form of faith is . . . I believe you; I believe in you", says an article in one of the post-Vatican-II Roman Catholic encyclopaedias,[49] perpetuating an ancient usage, perhaps by now anachronistic. Faith is always particular; and it lies in the realm of trust and loyalty among persons, of the giving of oneself and the finding of, being found by, the other. The word "believe" once designated that. To-day, on the other hand, it has come by a slow steady process to designate something else, in quite another realm, for all but a small minority.

This movement reflects, of course, general developments in modern Western civilization with its increasingly technocratic, thing-oriented outlook. The thought of that technocratic civilization in general, and modern logic in particular, have become adept at dealing with impersonal relations and instrumentally with the world of nature; but have grown notoriously poor, we increasingly realize, at dealing with the particular, and especially with persons, and most especially with interpersonal relations (and even with the natural world lovingly, reciprocally, with ecological and other wisdom). In this perspective, the history of the term "believe" emerges as not strange.

IV

We turn, finally, to the question of the relation of belief to truth—also historically envisaged. That relation, too, it turns out, has been slowly, steadily, changing. At issue here is not the truth or falsity of any specific belief, but the relation of believing as such to truth. This is the area of our third great shift in the usage of the word, over the past half-dozen centuries. Like the others, it has been major.

We may begin with a reference to the in some ways difficult and in some ways quite straightforward concept 'knowledge'. We all recognize that the word and notion "knowing" designate a certain relation of the mind to truth. One cannot "know" what is false; to know is to be both certain and right. We feel at ease with that, and it seems simple—until we raise the haunting question of how does one "know" anything; or until we notice that many persons in the past (at times including, alas, ourselves), and many still to-day, have thought that they knew, when in fact and in hindsight they were mistaken.

The word "to know" has meant, and means, to have an opinion that is correct, and to be aware that it is so; yet that very word has been used by people who were wrong. Now I ask that one perform with me a flight of fantasy. It is disconcerting to contemplate, but for a nimble fancy not impossible to imagine, that over the next some centuries things just might develop in such a way that the words "to know" and "knowledge" would come to mean "to think with firm conviction", whether right or wrong. If the established ideology of our civilization should turn out to seem less reliable than it was once held to be, if all its propositions should turn out to be deemed provisional, partial, or misleading, if it came to be felt that nobody does or in principle can really know anything in our present sense of the word (is your imagination sufficiently spry to indulge in this sort of dreaming?), or if another word came to serve to express this concept, then for the sake of argument one can presumably conjure up a situation where the words "to know" and "knowledge" in the English language could one day arrive at a point where they had lost their link with rightness, retaining only that with psychological assurance. I am of course not predicting that this will happen, and I hope that it will not; but an historian of language or of ideas can hardly rule it out as impossible. If a new ideology arose, with a differing basic theory of knowledge from our current one, then some other terms, such as perhaps "recognize" and "recognition", could take over the function of "knowing" and "knowledge" now.

My suggestion is that something of this sort has in fact happened with the notion "believing" over the past some centuries. It is possible, I find, to trace the steps by which this word, beginning by designating a certain relation to truth, gradually shifted through a region of neutrality and then uncertainty, where on the whole it stands to-day; though the movement continues towards a position closer, in fact, to falsehood, signs of its approaching which are beginning to be evident.

That is, the history of the word "believe" involves a gradual severing of its link with truth.

Suppose that someone asks me what is the population of Halifax. If I know, I will tell him. If I do not know, then I may say, "I believe that it is 175,000". I do not have to add to that: "... but I am not sure". The word "believe", even nowadays in the first person, has itself come to designate explicitly uncertainty and doubt. This was not always so. There was a time in English when believing added something to knowledge, rather than subtracting from it. In fact, the word designated a particular orientation to what one knows to be true.

Let us consider three statements, in modern English:

>   I. He recognizes that A is B.
> II. He is of the opinion that A is B.
> III. He imagines that A is B.

In the first case, the wording shows that he is right; in the last, that he is wrong; in the middle case, no stand is taken. There has been a tendency in English usage over the centuries for the words "belief", "believe" to shift from number I where they began, not only into II, but recently towards III. The evidence for this, as we shall see, seems clear.

Let us look at some examples.

We noted earlier that the noun "belief" occurs only once in the 1611 King James Authorized Version of the Bible. That occurrence is in the phrase "belief of truth" (II Thessalonians 2:13). The concurrence was significant. Besides, in twentieth-century English, "faith in truth", and indeed "fidelity to truth", would come closer to rendering the force; still closer would be in modern

German *das Belieben der Wahrheit*. For we shall see in our next chapter that it means allegiance to truth, clinging to it, commitment to what one knows to be true. "Belief" still has here its etymological and its mediaeval sense, of holding dear.

In Bacon, along with other later senses of the word, this one also is clear. Indeed, in his 1625 essay "Of Truth",[50] Bacon uses this same phrase; and explicates it. He enumerates three stages in man's dynamic relation to truth, which together constitute "the sovereign good of human nature". These are: "the inquiry of truth", "the knowledge of truth", and "the belief of truth"; in that order. The first of these, he says, is the wooing of truth; the second, the presence of it; the third, the "enjoyment of it". It is evident, then, that here belief is more than knowing. As in the Biblical English of 1611 it is a relation not to what is dubious but to what is true, and indeed to what is known to be true. Beyond that, it is a relation that adds something to knowing. What it adds is—that is, the word "belief" is the name for—appropriating that truth to oneself. The word "belief" is the name given to that further step of giving one's heart to what one's mind knows to be true (which, incidentally, is the Islamic theologians' leading definition of faith[51]): not merely recognizing it, but again in that etymological meaning of the term, holding it dear, delighting in it.

It is not insignificant, further, that in the next paragraph where Bacon passes "from theological and philosophical truth, to the truth of civil business", he again brings out that what he has in mind is the practice of truth, and not a mere knowing it. This practice of truth (or "clean and round dealing", which he calls "the honour of man's nature") he also speaks of as "faith" (he quotes the 1611 Bible with this term). It is contrasted with "the wickedness of falsehood" and "breach of faith", and with lying. Now this last is a matter not of not knowing the truth, but of a "perfidious" (to use one of his own terms here) turning from what one knows to be true. *Error* is the opposite of knowing what is true; *lying* is the opposite of "believing" what is true. For lying is the opposite of being faithful to it; it is disloyalty to truth. That is, the word "belief" still means "loyalty" here, as it repeatedly does in mediaeval English. Moreover, it is again a loyalty associated specifically with truth (just as the term "perfidy", from the Latin for anti-faith, or "false 'belief' ", is associated with lies).

With these illustrations of usage in mind we may go back a little and note certain instances in Shakespeare of this meaning of "belief" as fidelity to manifest truth. As we have seen, he uses "believe" primarily in the sense of trusting a person. When, secondarily, it has a proposition as object, it is almost always a proposition that the speaker considers true.[52] The stronger sense, however, of believing as active loyalty or adhesion to what is known to be true, is with Shakespeare a remnant only. Yet it is found. One instance is in *Macbeth* (4:3:9). "What [I] know, [I'll] believe", says Malcolm, meaning: I'll take seriously, will follow through with heart and hand, will do something about.[53] Similarly, when in *The Merry Wives of Windsor* (2:2:223) the disguised Ford says to Falstaff, "Believe it, for you know it", he means: You already know that it is true; make the further move of taking it to heart.

Another, more forceful, instance in Shakespeare where the mediaeval sense of "believing" as "maintaining staunch loyalty to" (something that is patently true) is found, is examined in our other study.[54]

It is not at once clear how much of this sense of fidelity to a truth that one knows is preserved in a sentence such as this of Hobbes: "the Beleef of this Article, *Jesus is the Christ,* is all the Faith required to Salvation".[55] Hobbes certainly presupposed that the article was true, and his phrasing could certainly still mean, as it had in earlier usage, a loyal commitment to its truth, an active adherence to it, an ordering of one's life in accord with it.

Insofar as there is in his discussion that follows an intellectualist and propositionalist emphasis, it is—in the sense developed in our next chapter below—one of "recognizing" a truth, rather than of believing in the modern sense which has to do with holding subjectively for true or probable what is objectively uncertain. This comes out, for instance, in the use presently of the word "know" as insouciantly equivalent.[56] Yet there seems to be something more. The role of the will—to good: as well as of the mind, to truth[57]—is here felt as not far distant; and "Beleef of this Article" evidently involves, in addition to such recognition, a following[58] through in practice, and the giving of one's allegiance.[59] Apart from this particular passage, we mentioned earlier his speaking elsewhere of believing a person; also, believing a doctrine, and may now note further that in those days "doctrine" meant teaching, including moral teaching, and not only a proposition.[60] Yet however this may be, in general insofar as propositional belief has begun in Hobbes it is primarily a believing of doctrines that are (or: of doctrine that is) true.

In the Middle Ages, we may recall, St. Thomas had explicitly said that the Latin words later translated as "believing"—namely, the verb *credere,* the noun *fides*—are only of what is true: if it is not true, then it is not *fides* (early English, belief).[61] Largely by the sixteenth and certainly by the seventeenth century, in English this is implicit only, not explicit. Yet implicit it is. When Bacon speaks of "belief and truth of opinion",[62] it could be either that the two are equivalent (so that "belief" in effect *means* "truth of opinion") or that, "belief" and "truth" once again forming a natural pair, the former connotes adherence, so that he means what in modern English would come out as valid views loyally held. Again, when he says that heathen religion has "no soul, that is, no certainty of belief",[63] he does not mean that its adherents have no firm beliefs in our sense and no convictions, of course. Rather, he is saying that what we would call their beliefs are lacking reliable truth. Their opinions do not lay hold upon a transcendent reality, and therefore are not to be called "belief".[64]

Echoes of the time when belief and truth as concepts were closely linked in either conscious or unconscious ways, can, I discover, be found well into the Enlightenment; not only with Locke in the late seventeenth century but even, surprisingly, in some ways with the skeptic Hume in the eighteenth. Hobbes had rejected the use of the word "belief" for an opinion that "we think probable . . . [and] admit for truth by error of reasoning", commenting of "belief" rather that it "in many cases is no less free from doubt, than perfect and manifest knowledge".[65] Locke tends to use the word "faith" for assent to propositions that are explicitly "above reason",[66] or are "highest reason"[67] and are "beyond doubt".[68] Of belief, assent, opinion, he writes positively as more or less equivalent, and thus with a certain neutrality (although their objects tend to come for him under such headings as "probability",[69] or "likeliness to be true", as befits his writing largely still in the first person plural[70]). On the other hand, while among these three words he writes of "wrong assent, or error", and of "erroneous opinions",[71] I have not found him using the phrase "false belief" or "wrong belief" as an explicit juxtaposition of terms[72]—though I may be wrong on this. I am not saying that by the turn of the seventeenth / eighteenth centuries he did not yet conceive of beliefs as such being potentially false. Clearly, he does so conceive. Hume so conceives with great liveliness, his unacceptance of Church theses being famous. Nonetheless the actual word "belief" for Hume does seem to have a certain positive resonance still; this is especially so, as one might expect, when he is speaking not of religious propositions but of human psychology in general.[73] In those discussions he introduces the first person plural, considering what is involved in the fact that we human beings "believe" some of our ideas in the sense of judging (or recognizing) them to be of the real world and not merely notions in our mind. Belief here is Stoic συγκαταθεσις [*synkatathesis*] (Latin: *adsensio, assentio*): that capacity of the mind to transcend its own ideas and to move from an awareness of an impression to an awareness of reality. (This ability to recognize the reality of that of which empirically we have only impressions, classically entered into definitions of faith.[74])

Thus Hume writes: ". . . the influence of belief is at once to inliven and infix any idea in the imagination, and prevent all kind of hesitation and uncertainty about it".[75] This contrasts with the twentieth century, when "believing" bespeaks hesitation, rather, and lowers certainty.

I do not, however, wish to exaggerate the matter on which I have here been touching. On the contrary, the point that I would urge is precisely that there has, indeed, been a steady and strong movement away from belief's connotation of truth. That connotation once was there, and for it I have a good deal more evidence than I have here presented, evidence that is overwhelming for the Middle Ages. Yet the important fact is that it gradually waned, from the sixteenth century; and while I have been surprised to discover how long it lingers in certain corners even among skeptical writers, I can without question at the same time document that in the seventeenth century and throughout the eighteenth and powerfully in the nineteenth, the tendency was towards not merely neutrality but eventually dubiousness. To say that "he believes A to be B" began by meaning that he recognizes this truth, but it came vividly to mean not only that perhaps he may be wrong, but that explicitly and conspicuously he may be wrong. Increasingly it came even to suggest that indeed he probably is wrong. Belief, once meaning trust, and adding something to knowledge, designating the difference between knowing inertly and knowing responsively, came increasingly to denominate rather a situation where lack of trust is in order. So-and-so knows that Canberra is the capital of Australia; so-and-so believes that Sydney is.

And eventually even of oneself. If—returning to our earlier illustration—I tell you that the population of Halifax is 175,000, I expect you to trust me. If, on the other hand, I say that I believe that it is that, I am indicating that I myself do not quite trust the figure and am suggesting that you too had better not trust it. "Please check it out before you rely upon it: it is a fallible estimate only."

My prize example of this trend is taken from the major recent Random House dictionary, published in New York in 1966. The first entry under the word "belief" defines it as "an opinion or conviction", and at once illustrates this with: *the belief that the earth is flat*".[76] What could be more casually devastating? The first example that comes to mind for the compilers, and then the readers, of this impressive work is a belief that is false. Is it not an eloquent illustration that the word has changed its meaning?

In fact, of this dictionary's four entries under our word, the illustration given for the first is false, the second "unworthy", the third childish, and the last religious.

And indeed, one would hardly use the word "belief" to-day for the view that the world is round, one realizes on reflection. In the late twentieth century we would hardly say, "He holds the belief that the earth is round". (The use of the verb would be slightly less absurd, but still odd.)

In other words, a primary association of our term is coming to be an association with ideas that are erroneous. The word denotes doubt, and connotes falsehood.

This has become so, even for the first person singular, with the result that it may connote then also insincerity. As Mark Twain reverberatingly put it in his posthumously published Notebook: " 'Faith is believing what you know ain't so' ".[77] This signifies a stage in linguistic evolution where even "I believe" has come to mean what "he believes" had eventually meant: the holding of a position that the speaker using our verb knows to be dubious.

In religious evolution it signifies a stage where some Christians seemingly came almost to imagine that salvation is by belief (rather than by faith, the divergent meaning of which had tended to get lost), so that some then tried to believe propositions for ulterior purposes. This understanding of religious life resulted in a caricature that would be grotesque were it not tragic.

We turn to another matter. It is under the perspective of this long-range historical transition—from truth, through neutrality, towards falsehood—that I personally would prefer to consider the question of believing in a person or in a single object, as well as the case that we have been observing with the double object, of a subject-predicate complex, the proposition. This single-object matter is usually treated these days, as we have remarked, as a distinction in the form of linguistic usage: as "believing in" over against "believing that". It is my general thesis that language is always secondary, both to that about which it speaks and to the person, the groups, the centuries that use it. Here too, then, one gains more insight, I would suggest, by attending to substantive matters.

We have seen that "believing" used to mean holding dear, esteeming, valuing highly, committing oneself to; and that the verbal expression conceptualizing one's act of so doing shifted its meaning over the centuries as the act's presupposition began to be called into question, and by many people dismissed. Attention then became focused not on the existential commitment of the subject but on the validity of the object. This is clearest as that object was or became propositional. A virtually parallel process can be discerned, however, with a single or simple object, the so-called "believe-in" pattern. Only, in that case it has proceeded somewhat more slowly.

To believe in God originally meant to dedicate oneself to Him, He being assumed to be there, and prior. It subsequently meant to recognize as true His statements, as we have quoted it meaning for Hobbes[78] (or His promises; or to recognize as obligatory His command). It has come to mean, to hold the opinion that He exists. This process has been a function of the predicate's being gradually called into question. This last stage appears linguistically in the eighteenth century. To believe in ghosts (cited from 1763[79]) means a belief that they exist, this having become dubious. An Englishman's belief in the sea, or in cold showers, on the other hand, is still in the twentieth century a matter of the subject's esteeming, valuing, since the object in these cases has not been eroded by doubt. So long as the presuppositions of a given valuation, or self-commitment, are not yet at issue, the word continues its earlier signification.

Thus the long-range process is the same in both instances. "Believe in" and "believe that" differ only in that they are to-day at differing stages in the same historical development—which they both illustrate.

An exemplifying entry in the Random House dictionary of 1966 of the belief-in usage is *"belief in astrology"*.[80] This bears pondering, as it is not at once lucid. It does not mean what "belief in ghosts" meant already two centuries ago. For here the existence of astrology is taken for granted; but its validity or usefulness is not. Yet there is, within this framework, an ambiguity still, since it is not clear without further elaboration whether the person who believes in astrology simply holds the view that this body of lore and of moods is what it claims to be, or also adds to that abstract judgement a moral decision, of existential participation, involving himself in them in his personal life and behaviour. It could be that he merely theoretically opines that the thing is sound, without himself doing anything about it; he might be intellectually interested only. Or, he may trust it; may entrust himself and his affairs to it. There was a time when the latter, only, would have been denoted by our word, but we are currently moving beyond that phase. Those who believe in abominable snowmen or in life in outer space have already passed it.

V

Where, then, have we arrived? In the course of this chapter we have been considering an historical period during which, of course, there has been at work a number of momentous forces: major movements in the evolution of Western civilization, the rise of natural science, the dominance of capitalism, the Enlightenment, the arrival of pluralism, and much else. I am suggesting that these mighty transitions are illustrated in shifts in usage of the apparently simple word "believe". I am further suggesting that these shifts of meaning have in fact proven of great consequence, especially for Christians, so deeply embedded has the term been in Christian thought, and so central; yet surreptitiously, so un-self-conscious has the development been. A change in the meaning of a key term has resulted in a fateful change of vision. It is one on which, it would seem, both theologians and so-called believers would do well to ponder. (It has also been of consequence for Western understanding—or failure to understand—the religious life of other communities: the faith of other men.)

Christian writers in English, naturally, have been affected by these various processes. I have found Wesley in the eighteenth century and Newman in the nineteenth, for example, particularly relevant and illuminating. It would constitute another study, however, to inquire into Christian theologians' involvement in, or their resistance to, the several developments, even at the linguistic level; and their adjustments to, compromises with, solutions for, the succession of problems arising. All this we leave aside, for some other occasion. (I might report that I have formed the impression that, on the whole, Protestant ecclesiastics have moved perhaps a century behind the more secular writers in their use of words—have maintained about a century longer traditional meanings—and Catholics perhaps a further century. Yet this is tentative.)

This one comment one might make, and with it we close: that modern Christian interest in religious belief (or: Christian belief) seems at times to have an almost adventitious air—to the point where one might wonder whether the concept "religious belief" (or, Christian belief) is not almost now a contradiction in terms.

The question of believing for Christians has received the emphasis that it has received, and has been tackled in the ways that it has been tackled, for almost no other reason, one might be tempted to imagine, than that the *word* "belief" used to be central for Christians when it designated something else.

In our opening section of this chapter it was remarked that theorists of religion seem perhaps to have been barking up a wrong tree. All the while the true tree has stood elsewhere, majestic but unattended: the tree of faith. We are now in a position, I can suggest, to understand how this tragicomedy of errors has come about. The historian discovers that the label previously on the tree of faith has been moved in modern times, to be affixed to this new tree. Philosophers, of course, are highly literate people, and pay much attention to labels. Theologians, though in this matter better dendrologists, are also much occupied with words: and some of them too have perhaps been mis-led by the switch. Yet this particular placard, inscribed in bold letters BELIEF, is a large and heavy one, not easily moved; and a conspicuous one, the focus of many eyes, so that it could be moved only surreptitiously. Accordingly, the shifting has required a good deal of time—some centuries, as we have seen—and the combined efforts of many strong men; and the move has had to be carried out quietly, virtually when no one was looking, a little at a time. Yet: carried out it has been. First, the venerable and highly treasured sign was gently moved to a neighbouring tree of basically the same species, then to one a little farther away but reasonably similar; and so by a series of small steps was eventually nailed to a quite different plant. The English "belief", which use to be the verbal sign designating allegiance, loyalty, integrity, love, commitment, trust and entrusting, and the capacity to perceive and to respond to transcendent qualities in oneself and one's environment—in short, faith; the Christian form of God's most momentous gift to each person—has come to be the term by which we designate rather a series of dubious, or at best problematic, propositions.

In our next chapter we shall look at the Bible, to see what light it can throw on these matters. In the meantime, one wonders.

III. The Bible

Belief as Non-Scriptural

IF FAITH IS not belief, what is it?—is a question on which we touch
here only briefly, leaving it rather to other occasions and to other
thinkers. Yet even with regard to the negative matter, that it is not
belief, one must reckon with the Bible, which to some has seemed
inescapably normative not only for Christian faith but for Christian
believing. It is bold even to consider a thesis that the Bible may not
speak about belief at all. Yet once a question is seriously pressed,
as to whether the concept actually occurs in its text, a number of
observations come to light that must be taken into account before
an answer can be given.

The considerations of our last chapter, and divers others, may
lead one to wonder whether the modern world has not in the literal
sense of the term mis-taken the concept belief, and quite mis-
conceived its role in religious life. Church thinkers, as well as
Muslims, Hindus, Buddhists, and certainly Jews, would agree that
faith is indeed the primary religious—that is, human—category.
Nonetheless, the relation of belief to it stands in need of radical
re-thinking. Creeds will have to be re-worded, once it is more
widely recognized that *credo* is mistranslated "I believe". So too, I
suggest, will the Bible, once what it has to say is scrutinized from
the new perspective.

Were the religious crisis of our modern world less serious, a
proposal would seem indeed too venturesome or too burdensome,
to re-translate the whole Bible so as to eliminate the words "belief",
"believe" from an English version. The crisis, however, is deep; and
one may wonder whether the time for this recasting has not come,
so misleading or at least ambiguous have these terms become. The
old translation is not merely wrong, but disruptive.

There are some facts to indicate that my interpretation is not
indeed quite so radical as it sounds. When I suggest that the
concept 'belief' does not occur in the Bible, I am supported by the
point, mentioned in our last chapter, that in the 1611 King James
Authorized Version in English the word "faith" occurs 233 times,

the word "belief" only once—in II Thessalonians 2:13; and even there, it does not in fact *mean* "belief". The *verb* "believe", on the other hand, occurs 285 times; and "believing", "unbelief", "believer", and other forms from this root bring these figures up to 321 (compared to 355 for the extended family of "faith" words: "faith" itself plus "faithful", "faithless", "faithfulness", etc.).[1] Now the first point to recall is that the translators generally chose "faith" for the concept involved wherever they reasonably could (with that one exception mentioned), settling for the older "believing" root only when pushed to it by the fact that unlike the Hebrew and Greek from which they were working (where the roots are אמן [*'-m-n, he^e mîn, ^e mûnāh*] and πιστις, πιστευω [*pistis, pisteuō*] respectively), English[2] has no verb to go along with the noun[3] "faith".

A second point is that more recent translations in English have in fact already dropped "believing" in some instances, usually for a construction with "faith" or some equivalent. One example is Romans 14:2, which in 1611 comes out as "believing that". "For one believeth that he may eat all things", while the New English Bible[4] gives ". . . one man will have faith enough to eat all kinds of food". In both cases the contrast is with the person "weak in the faith" (King James) or ". . . in his faith" (New English Bible): I would say, "weak in faith", of which more anon. In this case the 1611 version was in fact probably wrong already in its own time. A more amusing example is Job 39:24. Here the Hebrew reads יאמין [*ya^'a mîn*]; the subject is the horse. The 1611 translators gave: ". . . neither believeth he that *it is* the sound of the trumpet" ("it is" was in italics to show that that had been added). The Revised Standard Version reads: "he cannot stand still at the sound of the trumpet".

This illustration is not tendentious: for there is no doubt but that in general the Hebrew concept of faith has more to do with standing firm than it has to do with believing. Indeed, of the 320 occurrences of the אמן [*āman*] root in the Hebrew Bible, only 45 (or about one in seven) were translated by "believe" even in 1611; and even of this small group only one-ninth (one-eleventh, if one discount our horse) are "believing that"—not much more than one per cent of all occurrences.

It is the New Testament, however, as is well known, that

launched the concept 'faith' in a big way, as virtually a distinctive Christian category. The Greek word is πιστις [*pistis*], with the adjective πιστος [*pistos*], the verb πιστευω [*pisteuō*](once: πιστοω [*pistoō*]), and combined forms like ἀπιστος, ὀλιγοπιστια [*apistos, oligopistia*], etc.—in all, occurring an impressive 603 times in the New Testament (averaging well over once, or even twice, per page in most editions). Actually four per cent, I calculate, are followed by a "that" clause (*hoti* or accusative-and-infinitive) in the Greek; that is, have a proposition as object.

Clearly it is important for us to wrestle with the other passages, the overwhelming majority, where the object is not a proposition but, direct or indirect, is a thing or a person, and especially Christ and God; or where the word has no object. We shall turn to these presently. First, however, let me not evade that small, yet crucial, group of instances where the object of faith is expressed in a propositional statement. I have come to feel that even here a translation by "believing" is in the twentieth century misleading; not to say, wrong.

It is a common-place among New Testament scholars that the scriptural notion of faith is fiduciary, a trusting, entrusting of one-self, and also obedience, fidelity; and in other ways is more than intellectual. I propound nothing new in insisting on that. One could quote a number of secondary studies in support. "La foi, dans l'Evangile, ne signifie jamais la croyance" (Monnier[5]), "[N]owhere in the discourses of Jesus does the substantive [*sc.* πιστις (*pistis*)] denote conviction or belief. . . . It is trust rather than belief with which we are concerned in the life and teaching of Jesus" (Hatch[6]). For St. Paul faith is "not merely an intellectual assent to some proposition but a vital, personal commitment engaging the whole man . . . in all his relations with God, with other men, and with the world" (Fitzmyer[7]). And so on. Yet I do not pursue this, since my command of the secondary literature is not solid enough for me to make a judiciously balanced selection, and citations might amount to choosing evidence to buttress my case. The last quotation that I have given, however, from the Jerome Bible Commentary, 1968, is typical in that it is phrased, in standard twentieth-century fashion, "not *merely* an intellectual assent" (to some proposition) "but. . . ." In my submission, the word "merely" often could and should be dropped. It is not assent to a proposition, but is something else. The close relation between faith and obedience (πιστις [*pistis*] and ὑπακοη [*hypakoē*]) is much discussed, for instance.[8] Yet in a minority of cases, I agree, there is an intellectualist component, and we must consider this. Only after this has been treated shall we move on to the Biblically more central and decisive matters of personal faith.

I

To the general question of implicit presuppositions, the tacit conceptual framework within which the entire matter was presented, we shall attend presently; yet one facet of it arises at once. Meanwhile, therefore, let us look at cases where the propositions are explicitly spelled out. It would delay us too long, obviously, to look into each particular passage, relatively few though they be. Yet I think that even the most critical will regard it as fair if I choose for examination three verses that are, surely, decisive in this realm. One is James 2:19, rendered in 1611: "Thou believest that there is one God; thou doest well: the devils also believe, and tremble". The second are the words of Christ, as reported in St. John's Gospel, 13:19, to the disciples at the Last Supper: ". . . that . . . ye may believe that I am *he*". (Cf. John 8:24, etc.) The third is Hebrews 11:6: "without faith *it is* impossible to please *him*: for he that cometh to God must believe that he is, and *that* he is a rewarder of them that diligently seek him".

If in these three instances we can come to see that "believing that" is in the late twentieth century a mistranslation, it will probably be agreed that we are on to something.

Let us look at the first: those devils, who are said to believe, and to tremble.* This verse as a whole has been much discussed throughout Church history: it has constituted a famous lemma. The problem has always been, however, that this is the only instance in the whole Christian corpus where the word for faith

---

*The Greek[9] reads: συ πιστευεις ὁτι εἰς θεος ἐστιν; καλως ποιεις. Και τα δαιμονια πιστευουσιν και φρισσουσιν.—James 2:19.

seems to be used as an intellectual position without a following through on it. Normally, a certain sincerity was denoted by the term πιστευω [*pisteuō*], and throughout the Middle Ages in the Western Church by the Latin *credo* (etymologically, "I give my heart")—however prominent also the theoretical component in any position being taken. The words mean the embracing of that particular position and embracing along with it all its consequences. Added to the ideational stance is an existential involvement in its ramifying implications.

Probably we should say, a deliberate and positive existential involvement; for here also the devils are indeed existentially involved, in that φρισσουσιν [*phrissousin*] : they tremble. Their sense of God's existence is to them not merely an interesting fact, descriptively, but a threat. Nonetheless, they remain recalcitrant. Their response is not positive; and is not chosen. In this one verse, alone in the Bible, πιστευω [*pisteuo*] does not designate *faith*. In modern times it has been taken to represent, instead, simply belief. No wonder it has agitated the commentators.

One may adduce in this connection the terms ὁμολογεω and ὁμολογια [*homologeō, homologia*], "to confess" and "confessing", a fairly frequent concept in the New Testament; and its opposite ἀρνεομαι [*arneomai*], "to deny". The former, with its counterparts, Latin *confiteri, confessio,* German *bekennen, Bekenntnis,* and the English "confess, confession", have had a major history. We speak of confessing the Lord Jesus Christ, of the Confessional Churches, and the like, and also of confessing a crime. The point in both cases is that one affirms a theoretical position and at the same time voluntarily takes on, accepts fully for oneself, the consequences. To know that one has committed a crime is one thing; to confess it normally includes the former but goes far beyond it. The case is similar with ἀρνεομαι [*arneomai*] "to deny", another cardinal Christian concept; specifying what Peter did at Christ's trial,[10] and later, unfortunately, what Peter accused the Jews at large of,[11] thus laying the basis for anti-Semitism. It is very clear that this word does not mean to be ignorant; nor, to disbelieve. On the contrary, it denotes the repudiating of what one knows. Both "to confess" and "to deny", in Church usage, presupposed belief in our modern sense. This is so, despite or along with the fact that with only the former term, of course, is πιστευω [*pisteuō*] regularly correlative. As in the Qur'an case,[12] so in the Bible, one believes, in the modern sense, both what one accepts and what one rejects.

The act of faith and the act of confession have much in common; even, at times, are synonymous. The act of rejecting, of denying one's Lord—important among Christians in the era of the fierce persecutions of the Church—was significant only because with it, too, belief in our modern sense went along. (In both the Islamic and the Christian instances, what was heinous was not the denial of the world-view; rather, what made denial heinous, and indeed what made it denial, was acceptance of the world-view.)

The peculiarity of the wording of our verse in James, where the devils πιστευουσι [*pisteuousi*] but tremble, is that they deny in practice what they recognize theoretically as valid. In their heart and their behaviour they reject what their mind accepts.

I am acknowledging, then, of course, as one must, that in this particular verse, perhaps alone in the Bible, πιστευω [*pisteuō*] does not mean "to have faith". I am suggesting, however, that neither does it mean "to believe". My point will be clear, I think, because of our considerations in our last chapter.

The reader will recall that we listed there three positions:

    I. He recognizes that A is B.

    II. He is of the opinion that A is B.

    III. He imagines that A is B.

Further, it was submitted that the English "believe" used to signify number I, that it has come to signify II, and is moving towards III. I now suggest, accordingly, that in our day the only way to translate our three Biblical passages is somewhat as follows. St. James: "You recognize God's oneness? Good! But the devils also recognize, and tremble". Christia: "... in order that you may recognize that I am He". Hebrews: "He that comes to God must recognize that He exists. ..."

Let us elaborate this a little. First, in accord with my own principles, our three model statements require personalizing, for strict analysis. It is important, who makes them. Accordingly we

---

*ἰνα πιστευσητε ... ὃτι ἐγω εἰμι.—John 13:19.

may set down the three positions more fully and more technically, as follows:

    I. Mr. X reports that M recognizes that P.
    II. Mr. Y reports that M is of the opinion that Q.
    III. Mr. Z reports that M imagines that R.

In the first case, we may say (and did in effect say, previously) that entailed in this language is that the opinion P is correct. This might better be refined by saying not only that it is correct, but that M knows it to be correct, *and so does Mr. X reporting.* On the other hand, since knowledge is a tricky matter, a still further refinement would be to say that number I is the normal way of speaking when both X and everyone who hears or reads the sentence feels quite sure that P is correct. Thus, it would be reasonable to say: Mr. X reports that M recognizes that the earth is round.

In number II, Y takes no stand as to whether Q be true or false. The strength or vehemence of M's opinion is altogether irrelevant here. So, too, is its correctness. Q may be right; but if M is not fully sure, and even more, if Y is not fully sure, then this is the standard phrasing.

Similarly with III. The wording here entails that Z holds R to be false. It implies, further, that those who receive the report (listeners, readers) agree.

Let us introduce now an historical dimension. Our "X reports that M recognizes that the earth is round" is good twentieth-century talk. If we go back to the sixteenth century, however, one may readily suppose a Mr. Z reporting that Copernicus imagines that the earth goes round the sun. (Philipp Melanchthon was one such; and in the following century, Francis Bacon took a comparable stand.[13]) In this case again, the strength of M's holding the opinion is quite irrelevant; as is also its truth or falsity. We to-day know that Copernicus was right.[14] It has been disputed whether he himself "knew" it: how far he felt sure of his case, or simply regarded his theory as an hypothesis, as he himself termed it in the preliminary résumé[15] which he circulated about 1514 or so. So long as Melanchthon or others thought him wrong, however, and felt that their audiences would surely concur, they would use our sentence III.

It should be remarked, however, that although "to imagine"(or:

to fancy, to suppose) is here appropriate, "to believe" is not inappropriate, and is becoming less so. It is less illuminating, it describes less accurately the total situation than does the more pejorative verb—except for very modernized readers. Nonetheless, even for an older generation, it does serve. In the twentieth century, we may say that so-and-so imagines that the earth is flat; or, *à la* Random House dictionary, that he believes it.

Now my argument here is that the three scriptural passages that we have noted come under heading I. It is therefore in our day (unlike 1611) a mistranslation to render them with "believe". The writer in each case, and those whom he expected to be his readers, were themselves very sure that God exists. In James's case this is quite explicit. You, he says in so many words, recognize God's existence; as do I; as do the devils. This recognition of the truth, however, without the addition of operative faith, is, he wishes to say, not enough. This is the case also for the Christian Church that made this letter of James part of its scripture, and among whose members it then circulated for many centuries. They were quite sure of God's existence. It is not that they thought of it as an opinion that they held, even one the probability of whose accuracy might be high. On the contrary, God was for them the ground of all knowledge. Twentieth-century persons may disagree with them (as we may disagree with Melanchthon and Bacon): but in the first century and for many a century thereafter their position could be described, and indeed can be accurately described only, as coming out of what they regarded as knowledge.

It distorts St. John's Gospel to hear him as presenting a Christ saying that he hopes that his followers will develop a certain opinion about himself. Whether the historical Jesus actually uttered these words is not at issue; but it is a mistranslation of John's Greek to read him differently. For John, and for the Christ whom he presents, it is a question of recognizing.

On the other hand, I think that there is no question but that many modern readers, and perhaps particularly skeptics such as analytic philosophers, when confronted with a statement such as our Hebrews verse in the King James Authorized Version, understand the phrase ". . . believe that God exists" as saying, and they read it as saying, ". . . imagine that God exists". Given their own presuppositions, this is almost inescapable. All that I am saying is that *this is not what the text originally affirmed.* They have misunderstood the sentence. To render it in words that in modern English communicate this level-III idea is to mistranslate the passage.

"To believe" in modern English means to hold an opinion, whether it be right or wrong. (Increasingly, it means to hold an opinion that is at best dubious.) No serious theological thinker has ever held, and the Bible nowhere suggests, that it is important to hold the opinion that God exists, whether that opinion be right or wrong.

Belief, in the modern meaning of the word, has had no place in the history of Christian thought. *The concept is not in the Bible.*

Some might suppose that I am being precious: that the Biblical writers may have been sure of what they were talking about, but we to-day are not, and therefore, we cannot get away from the "believing" concept. I contend that this has nothing to do with the matter. You and I may not believe in devils; but this is no reason for our not translating James accurately when he writes of them. We do not insidiously revise his text to make it conform to our notions of deviltry or non-deviltry. Neither should we similarly distort what he says about their attitude.

The word for "devils" is in his text; a word for "believe" is not. Indeed, if one thinks about it, one will realize that it is a contradiction in terms to say that devils imagine God to exist; or even that they believe it. Either there are no devils; or else, they recognize. (Even if one conjures them up, one has to imagine them as recognizing.[16])

It is not to be supposed that the point that I am making is trivial; or is merely linguistic. Faith precedes belief. To have reversed this order is a modern, and a tragic, heresy. Let us consider a little more closely that verse from Hebrews,* which at first blush seems to support the heresy, but in my view contradicts it.

"Without faith it is impossible to please him: for he that cometh to God must πιστευσαι [*pisteusai*] that he is, and that he is a

---

* Χωρις δε πιστεως ἀδυνατον εἰαρεστησαι, πιστευσαι γαρ δει τον προσερχομενον τῳ θεῳ ὁτι ἐστιν και τοις ἐκζητουσιν αὑτον μισθαποδοτης γινεται.—Hebrews 11:6.

rewarder of them that diligently seek him." I would wish to argue, with whatever force I could muster, that no one should believe in God who has not personally encountered Him. I would plead with you in the name of all that is holy to believe only what you see, and to believe in God only insofar as you see Him and know Him, dimly or vividly, or can discern His acting in history or in your own life and can perceive or sense His presence in the world, at least in its more lovely parts, or in persons, or on a cross. Rather than first believing that He exists and only then coming to Him, I would insist that true religious faith requires that we proceed the other way 'round: that we must first come to Him and only then believe in Him.

Anything else is disloyal, dishonest, and disruptive. It is disloyal to Him, dishonest to ourselves, disruptive of faith itself. And it has been throwing into disarray the modern Church.

Faith is a radically divergent thing from belief. And it has become disastrous to confuse the two. Belief follows after faith, and theology is simply an honest human attempt to conceptualize, in the terms of one's day, the faith that one has priorly had, the vision that one has seen. This is radically more healthy than the notion that has gained ground in Western society that one must *first* believe, in order to have faith; that believing is the price that one must pay. If there be any entrance fee for faith, this is not it—as sensitive and honest souls in our modern world have deeply known or felt.

Over against this, it would not be too fanciful to think of faith as in the first instance insight. Faith at this level is the capacity to see.

It is the capacity to see for oneself the loveliness of what is lovely; to see the difference between justice and injustice; to see the stupendous importance of truth; to see the point of a cup of cold water given in love, or the point of a man dying on a cross. If we see what is there waiting to be seen in our life and in this strange world of ours, waiting not necessarily on the surface but just beyond it, and then more, beyond that, then we have faith. If we see even a little, we soon find that there is more and more. If we do not see, if we see nothing beyond the surface at all, which is life's supreme tragedy, then we do not have faith. Faith in God is the ability to see God—first somewhere, finally perhaps everywhere.

And what about our text? Looked at more closely, it affirms the very thing that I am saying here; although this is obscured to us to-day by the 1611 translation, perpetuated also in perhaps all modern versions, alas. Without faith it is impossible to please Him. And anyone who comes near to God must have faith, must have been able to see for himself that God is there, and have seen His rich rewarding of those whose lives are a quest for the divine, rather than for any mundane or selfish advantage.

If one does not realize, has not recognized, that the universe that we live in has coherent transcendent qualities in it which have been called divine, and that these are more worthwhile, more rewarding, than anything else that one can pursue, then one will not get close to the reality of those qualities. This is faith: the recognition of worth.

This is what the text in Hebrews is asserting.

I remarked, however, that the passage in James that we cited is the only occurrence in all Christian literature where the recognition at issue is inert. Faith, insofar as its intellectual component is concerned, is recognition, insight, the capacity to discern. To this intellectual component, however, is added here in Hebrews and elsewhere throughout Christian literature another: that of commitment. There is involved the self-engagement of giving oneself to what one sees as worthwhile; the active adhesion to the truth that one has perceived. Socrates held that knowledge of the good inherently includes a pursuit of it. St. Paul would seem vehemently to disagree.[17] For him something additional is requisite: namely, faith. In any case, it is clear that the early Church, and classical Christian usage, stressed that faith is recognition plus response. It adds something to armchair knowledge. Πιστις, πιστευω[*pistis, pisteuō*] never mean less than "to recognize". Usually they mean more ("knowledge" plus "acknowledge").

II

We may pursue this aspect by moving now to our second sub-heading: of passages where the concept of faith is followed not by a proposition, a complex or double object, of subject and predicate, but by a single one; where the object is a thing. Let us remind ourselves that statistically this pattern is somewhat more common in the New Testament than with a "that" clause such as we have considered; though both taken together are a good deal less common than either of the cases that we shall be considering next, when the object, direct or indirect, is a person; or when there is no object.

The single object, as we noted also earlier with the English language, is sometimes a person's word, statement, report—which is transitional between the propositional object, on the one hand, and on the other hand the personal, to which we shall come next. These present no new principles (even if, once again, faith in a promise be noteworthy). When the object is non-verbal, however, there are considerations that arise. The first passage to which we turn, as illustrative, is II Thessalonians 2:10-13, one part of which we earlier noted in passing as the one instance where the noun "belief" got into the King James English, though for modern times misleadingly. In the four verses here in the Greek the verb occurs twice and the noun once; although there is actually a symmetry, with the correlative noun ἀγαπη [agape] , "love", also once. The context is one in which the author (perhaps St. Paul?) is setting forth a conflict between the Truth and the Lie, in a way strongly reminiscent of Persian dualism with these two as cosmic forces. He speaks in eschatological terms of the Wicked One whom Christ will slay; and sets up a sharp contrast between "those who are to perish" on the one hand and "you, brethren beloved by the Lord" whom "God chose . . . from the beginning to be saved".[18] The former will perish "because they refused to love the truth* and so be saved". 'Therefore God puts them under a delusion, which works upon them to' *have faith in the Lie,* † 'so that they may all be brought to judgement, all who do not' *have faith in, opt for, give their allegiance to* 'the Truth but make sinfulness their deliberate choice'. It is over against these that the Christians to whom the letter is addressed are said in the next verse to be loved by God and saved "through sanctification by the Spirit and" *faith* "in the Truth".

---

* τὴν ἀγαπην της ἀληθειας [tēn agapēn tēs alētheias] —II Thess. 2:10.

† το πιστευσαι τῳ ψευδει [to pisteusai tōi pseudei] —verse 11.

For one thing, there is the direct verbal parallel here between love of the truth (verse 10: just cited) and faith in the truth* (verse 13). More generally, it is quite evident that the point at issue is where one puts one's allegiance, where one gives one's heart, to which of these two contrasting forces one consecrates one's life. Πιστευειν τῳ ψευδει [*pisteuein tōi pseudei*] means to align oneself with the Lie, to enlist in its (his) service, to devote one's living to it. The parallel† is, "had pleasure in unrighteousness". There is no question here of mere intellectual error. (For most modern readers, a rendering "believe what is false" is simply wrong, if I may say so with due respect to the modern translators.) It is a matter, rather, of delighting in a Lie, of taking pleasure in what one knows to be false. The sense of recognition is at work also here, in that the implication is clear and intentional that these men knowingly choose deception.

Similarly with faith in Truth. (The capital T here, also the capital L with the Lie, are surely appropriate: a comparative historian familiar with the Persian material could hardly resist those majuscule initials.) Πιστις ἀληθειας [*pistis alētheias*] means a clinging to truth, a self-committing allegiance to its imperious claims upon us; a decision. As we saw in our last chapter, this is how Francis Bacon understood it. A wording "faith in truth" still preserves to-day more of this flavour. "Fidelity to truth" as we observed there, comes still nearer, as a modern rendering; although even it may connote less activism. The issue is that of taking sides in a monumental, a cosmic, option involving the totality of one's person: one's life and behaviour here on earth and as well, explicitly, one's eternal destiny.

The presentation here is dramatic. Yet, drama or no, the point is a solid one, of pervasive significance. The love of, or dedication of oneself to, truth as a final good has played an impressive role in human history, as well as being important in everyday routine. It bears reflection.

Many modern philosophers, having lost their hold upon trans-

---

*πιστει ἀληθειας [*pistei alētheias*] —verse 13; cf. οἱ . . . πιστευσαντες τῃ ἀληθειᾳ [*hoi . . . pisteusantes tēi alētheiai*] —verse 12.

†εὐδοκησαντες τῃ ἀδικιᾳ [*eudokēsantes tēi adikiai*] .

cendence, tend to be more interested in extant truth, truth as known, than in subtle and searching questions about the human relation to transcending truth. This relation expresses itself in the pursuit of truth not yet discovered, the love of something not now empirically real. Locke, for instance, at the turn of the seventeenth/ eighteenth centuries, still regarded it as "the principal part of human perfection in this world".[19] Faith in our explicitly religious traditions is a person's relation to, love of, attraction by, God or ultimate reality, or, as the scholastics called it, primordial truth (*prima veritas*—Aquinas), a relation that on earth is awaiting a perfect consummation in heaven. The counterpart in our Western philosophic and academic tradition is this love of truth not yet known.

As I have put it on another occasion, love of truth that is known may make a man a fanatic; love of truth not yet discovered makes him an intellectual. The dedication of one's life to the pursuit of transcendent truth, plus the moral commitment to order one's life in accord with such truth as one can here approximate, is this πιστις [*pistis*] in New Testament Greek. It used to be called "belief" in English; and then "faith"; Locke called it "love" of truth (one may recall that "believe" and "belove" were originally the same word). (Ayer perhaps has no name for it: I find it rather sad that he ends his Gifford Lectures with a note that what we might call the pursuit of truth is interesting.[20])

Let me quote Locke more fully on this. His wording is almost casual; yet worth noting is how saturated it all is with notions of transcendence, and of human orientations to it. "He that would seriously set upon the search for truth", he writes in a chapter added to the fourth edition of his *Essay concerning Human Understanding*,[21] "ought in the first place to prepare his mind with a love of it. For he that loves it not, will not take much pains to get it; nor be much concerned when he misses it." "[T]here are very few lovers of truth, for truth's sake", he goes on a little later. And in the letter to a friend, Anthony Collins, from which I have already quoted, written in 1703, he writes: "To love truth for truth's sake is the principal part of human perfection in this world, and the seed-plot of all other virtues".[22] These are faith statements. A comparative religionist quickly recognizes them as that—and applauds. Yet like other faith-statements around the world they are ones that a linguistic analyst might find, I suppose, strictly meaningless? How can one love what one has not yet found? Faith is the human orientation to transcendence.

After Locke's death, Lady Damaris Masham wrote about him to a mutual friend: "He was always, in the greatest and in the smallest affairs of human life, as well as in speculative opinions, disposed to follow reason . . .; he being ever a faithful servant—I had almost said a slave—to Truth".[23] "A faithful servant, . . . a slave, to Truth" is an idea worth pondering. Truth was his God; and this faithful service was perfect freedom.

This is the sort of matter at issue in the Biblical concept πιστις [*pistis*]. When the English word "belief" meant that, no wonder belief was important. But it is hardly the right translation in English for it to-day.

Apart from truth, another thing-object for faith in the New Testament is love. For our purposes I John 4:16 is interesting both because it has την ἀγαπην [*tēn agapēn*]—self-giving love—as the direct object of the verb πιστευω [*pisteuō*], and also because this verb follows directly after, and supplements, the verb "to know", thus illustrating once again that what is at issue here is something not less than knowledge, but more than it, including it: but going beyond. Far from signifying opinion, it designates that activating move that transforms theoretical knowing into knowing plus sincerity. The Greek is ἐγνωκαμεν και πεπιστευκαμεν [*egnō kamen kai pepisteukamen*]. The translation "know and believe", though still in use, is awkward English. Nowadays, one does not "know and believe" anything, in that order.

The latter part of this verse is the famous and magnificent: "God is love, and he who abides in love abides in God, and God abides in him". The opening part of the verse (following upon "we know", "we have seen", "we are witnesses" in the preceding verses: there is nothing here about conjecture) affirms, "We have come to know the love that God has in us" and adds πεπιστευκαμεν [*pepisteuka-men*]), meaning that in response we have dedicated ourselves to live in terms of that love. Not only do we know it: more, we accept it, and give ourselves over to it; we orient our lives henceforth in alignment with it. This is the decision (or capacity) to live in terms of what one knows to be good.

Once again, there is expressed here no element of believing (in to-day's sense) at all. Not a whiff of it. There is no trace of it; not the merest hint of a suggestion of it.

III

We come, next, to the standard use of our verb: with a personal object, whether direct, indirect, or via a preposition. By the way, I include God and Christ in the category of 'persons'. If any be tempted to feel that we are being metaphorical in that, let me recall the argument that the truth of the situation may be seen, rather, as *vice versa*: that Western civilization has come to regard people as persons metaphorically, the concept being metaphysical, and proper first (historically and logically) to God—especially as Son, but also as Father, and Spirit. We get our word and concept 'person' in large part from the doctrine of the Trinity[24]—our perceiving of each other as persons being the product of our recognizing (again I use that word) a transcendent quality, ultimately a divine image, behind the empirical facade of each other's outward form and behaviour.

That faith in the Bible is primarily in persons is a comment not only on the Christian contribution to our conception of faith, but also on that to our conception of humanity, of personhood. The concept 'person' is, *inter multa alia*, of that that is an object of faith. Nor is this in any way whimsical. If no one has faith in a particular person, that individual will have trouble in becoming or remaining a person, as the psychiatrists well know.

There is a further general point about faith being presented in the New Testament as largely a matter of faith in persons. How many of us lie awake at night thunderstruck that we human beings can trust each other, be loyal to each other? It is worth being impressed by, and wondering hard and long how it comes about. Durkheim derived religion from society; being Jewish, he took social cohesion for granted. Today, alas, we know better. He spoke much sense; but one could equally well turn his thesis around and affirm that faith is what turns a society into a community. It is the cause, and not only the result, of corporate solidarity of persons.

Let us turn from the generic to the particular. We begin with faith in God; but need pause but briefly, after what was said just now about faith in the Truth, and in our last chapter, about erstwhile English "I believe in God". *Credo* in God means much; beginning with, "I pledge myself to live in loyalty to Him; I hereby align my life, my behaviour, my mind and heart and soul, with His will for me; I consecrate and entrust myself to His love, justice, mercy, power. . . ." Yet one may be haunted by the presuppositional bugbear. *Credo* may be a performative, *à la* Austin, may be existential, *à la* the Continent, but does it not evaporate unless it be undergirded by a descriptive, propositional postulate that God *is*? We shall return to this presuppositional matter later. For the moment I only ask that if need be, one use one's imagination a little.

In the comparative study of religious history we are so accustomed to performing for other cultures in Asia and elsewhere the requisite imaginative act of reconstructing in our minds the ideational and terrestrial milieu in which the persons that we study once lived, the actions that we study once took place, that it becomes second nature to us; and I keep forgetting how troublesome an issue this apparently can be for others not so blessed. Let me merely remind ourselves, however, that to presuppose the existence of God is necessary only if we personally are to pronounce the formula. Just now all that we are doing is attempting to understand what other people meant when they pronounced it; specifically, to understand their use of the words πιστευω and πιστις [*pisteuō, pistis*] in the New Testament. We do not have to believe in God to appreciate the fact that when they used these concepts they were not talking about believing in God either, but about something else. It is a sub-hypothesis of mine that if one comes to understand what they meant when they talked this way, how they felt, what they saw, what they purposed, how they ordered their personalities, then one will begin to understand what faith is, and begin also then to realize that belief has essentially relatively little to do with it—or anyway, less to do with it than we used to think: not only those persons' believing, but one's own not believing. One does not have to adopt the Islamic world-view to appreciate Muslims' faith; nor the Buddhist, to appreciate Buddhists'.

That, however, I toss out only in passing. All that I am saying at the moment is that believing as a concept is not salient here; and am endeavouring to remind us what is. There is no reason why a Jew or a Hindu, who does not believe or plan to believe the Christian doctrines, should not move towards a vivid appreciation of what πιστις, πιστευω [*pistis, pisteuō*] meant in the Bible, and what faith then meant in the lives of these early Christians, and what *credo* meant in mediaeval centuries.

Faith as trust has, of course, been much canvassed, especially by Protestants; and since we all know pretty much what it means to trust a person, and to be oneself trustworthy (even if we do not quite understand them), we need not delay over that aspect. In the realm of statistics I do not know whether others will find it of as much interest as did I to learn that the occurrences of the adjective πιστος [*pistos*] (trusting, trsutworthy, loyal, faithful; person of faith; reliable statement or thing) are 71 in all, of which 8 are of things, chiefly verbal things, 14 are of God and Christ, 49 of human beings. In passing, also, I find it of interest—in fact, revealing: casting bright illumination on the human condition—that also in Chinese,[25] as in Greek, the same word means both trusting and trustworthy. To be a person who trusts others, and to be a person whom others may trust, co-incide. Is our society to-day wrong in thinking of these as two different acts, two distinct qualities?

The person in the New Testament who is primarily the focus of faith and the centre of the new concept is, of course, Christ. Many writers have set forth this, and I have nothing new to add—except perhaps once again to subtract, rather, a matter of believing anything; and to substitute, at the propositional level, the thesis about recognizing. The Christian movement arose not as a body of persons who believed that Jesus was the Christ, but as an upsurge of a new recognition in human history: a sudden new awareness of what humanity can be, is, all about; the dawning of a new insight into what what had previously been called divine could, and should, be understood as meaning (God is not simply high and lifted up, in the sanctuary; He is a carpenter in a small town . . .); a new recognition of human potentialities, one's own, one's neighbours, the proletariat's, the drunkard's. Participants in this movement did not think that they believed anything. And while their new vision of the world and of themselves was articulated in quite an array of new conceptual symbols, I am not sure that an historian wishing to apprehend what was going on should concentrate on those symbols, except as clues to something much deeper and more personal. It is not what they believed that is significant, but the new faith that the belief-system gave a pattern to, and was generated by.

In any case, faith was primarily in a person, not in a doctrine. Certain fundamentalist groups in the United States still to-day make a point of the phrasing, Believe "on" the Lord Jesus Christ, and be saved; apparently (perhaps unconsciously) to stress this very issue, of the non-doctrinal. After A.D. 30 or so the faith was on the figure of a person, rather, it might be contended: the figure of Christ. Yet skeptics who urge that the faith of the Church was and has been on an imaged or ideal figure, not an actual person, may be reminded once again that the concept 'person' is ideal (to use Greek terms), divine (to use Palestinian), not empirical. How else could we talk of becoming a real person, or of depersonalizing forces, or the like? How else could we know that there is more to us and to each other than we think, than meets the eye? On this matter I do have a new point to make, not primarily about the text of the Bible itself as a first-century document but about the period since. It has to do with the role of the Bible in the course of the many centuries after the first. It is the view, once again, of an historian and one that sees history as an on-going process. I am not that kind of historian who sees his task as getting always back to origins, dismissing the subsequent; I am at least equally interested historically in the ever-changing development of anything after it first arose.

At the turn of the present century a polarity was posited in the English phrase "The Jesus of history or the Christ of experience"; or in another wording, ". . . the Christ of faith".[26] This goes back to a German debate earlier between Strauss[27] and Schleiermacher; it grew out of the historical-criticism movement of the nineteenth century, of course. My suggestion is that we are perhaps ready now for a new and more realistic polarity, which one might entitle (I have thought to write an article some day, under this heading), "The Christ of history, and the historical Jesus of a certain type of turn-of-the-century faith". The point to be made would be that it is the Christ figure of continuing faith in the on-going life of the Church that has in actual historical fact been primarily significant, operative, consequential. This is where empirical truth primarily lies. It is here that the historian of religion should be primarily interested; or, say, a Japanese Buddhist or Indonesian Muslim or the like wishing to understand either Christian religious matters or Western civilization (or the human situation). If one felt provocative, one might sum up such a thesis in the aphorism: the Jesus of History is a rather shadowy figure; the Christ of faith has been historically real.

If God has been active in history—and *pace* the analysts, that is a form of poetry that I see no reason for even them to shun—then in Christendom He has been so, strikingly, through that ever contemporary figure of Christ moving down the centuries, and the faith that men and women have had in Him.

One does not have to be a Christian to recognize (*sic*) that faith; and indeed to recognize it as among the monumental facts of human history.

(Call that figure of Christ imaginary if you will: scientists, if not philosophers, know well that it takes imagination to grasp any truth that is not stale; Hindus, if not other types of theologian, have long recognized that God can use people's imagination to save them through awareness of truth; the European Romantic poets elevated imagination into a capacity for apprehending realities that can be reached no other way. To call it imaginary simply in the sense of 'untrue' is to postulate and to subscribe to a metaphysical doctrine for which the evidence is hardly adequate.)

IV

We turn now to the most frequent pattern of all in the New Testament, for the concept 'faith': namely, where it is used absolutely; with no object. The fact that this is the most common usage, and this usage itself, have received less notice from scholars, theologians, philosophers, Christians. It seems to me to deserve, to demand, attention. Also, to reward it. Let us go back to statistics. There are 246 occurrences of the noun πιστις [*pistis*] in the Greek New

Testament; 29 times with an object in the genitive, or with the prepositions εἰς, ἐν, ἐπι, προς [*eis, en, epi,* and *pros*] ("Faith into, in, on, upon, to"). In 217 cases, however, or 88 per cent of the time, it occurs alone.

With the verbs the percentage is significantly lower, though still impressive: this usage accounts for a little over one-third of all instances.[28] The privatives "of little faith", "lack of faith" [*oligopistos, apistia*] and the like, are entirely so.

The fact is that in the New Testament, faith is a quality or an activity regularly set forth as something in and of itself, not as explicitly directed to an object. Put blankly, this fact may seem startling. In context, usage is less so, even to our modern ears. "When the son of man comes, will he find faith on earth?" "Oh ye of little faith!" "Thy faith hath made thee whole." "And now abideth faith, hope, charity, these three. . . ." "By faith Abraham . . . obeyed. . . . Through faith . . . Sara. . . . By faith Moses. . . ."[29] This continued standard for centuries.[30] A thousand five hundred years later Luther took this up and proclaimed salvation by faith.

Many moderns will immediately respond by ejaculating, "But of course they *meant* faith in Christ!" (or: ". . . in God"; or, in. . .) . I have found it good practice not to be hasty in assuming that writers in the past necessarily meant what we would mean (especially when they did not say it!). Certainly it would seem that any of us who might wish to develop the concept of faith as a generic quality—as comparative historians of religion are pushed towards doing—would have more foundation to build on, in the New Testament, than is usually recognized. The standard Christian position, however, in recent times has been to interpret these facts in subordination to the other instances. It is taken for granted, and if challenged it would be argued, that the minority usage—with one or another object—is 'of course' determinative, and that whenever no object is expressed, one of these is to be supplied.

I have some reason to suspect that this view has become standard only since Schleiermacher, who stands at the beginning of the era in which it has gradually come to be recognized that a Christian form of faith, through Christ, is one form of faith among others. He published in 1818 the first book ever on specifically Christian faith.[31] Previously, Christians had not known that there was any other kind. (Some still do not.) My investigations on this matter, however, are incipient. Anyway, nowadays it is normally held that especially "faith in Christ" but also "faith in the Gospel", "faith in God", "faith that . . .", and the like, are foundational; and that wherever "faith" is used alone, one or another object is tacitly understood. There has hardly yet been a reckoning with the possibility that this is a modern theological judgement read into the New Testament out of present-day orientations and conceptual presuppositions, rather than read out of it. Given recent religious understandings, it is of course not easy to hear it any other way.

In Acts, for instance, when the record states that "a great multitude both of the Jews and also of the Greeks πιστευσαι [*pisteusai*]" (Acts 14:1), which might be rendered "found faith", this is translated as "they believed", and is understood as meaning that they believed the Gospel, or believed the κηρυγμα [*kērygma*], or believed in the Lord, and so on. Some object, direct or indirect, person or thing or proposition, is tacitly read in. Doubtless, this is plausible.

It is plausible also, if slightly less so, with St. Paul's letter to Romans, which is a great paean on faith as such. Of the several dozen occurrences of both noun and verb, 76 per cent are absolute. Yet, it is regularly nowadays interpreted as signifying faith in this or that.

Least plausible are the Gospels, where the word for faith is on Christ's lips twenty or thirty (even forty) times: once of faith in God, otherwise always with no object.[32] Certainly for Christ, faith was something by which a person is characterized less or more: "I have not found so great faith, no, not in Israel", "Faith as a grain of mustard seed", and so on.[33] This appears to have been the case also with those who heard him. "Lord, I have faith: help my lack of faith" (Mark 9:24). It seems evident that for Jesus, faith was a quality of the person, rather than any externalized viewing.

On the other hand, the major New Testament scholar Oscar Cullmann not long ago published a small book precisely to argue that, in the early Church, faith means faith in Christ.[34] I find it curious but instructive to notice how, in this case and often, faith is indeed defined in terms of its object; as if everyone knew what faith is, and all we need to ascertain in any given case is, where it is directed. Indeed, if one read Cullmann's book carefully, one finds that he does not in fact ask what faith was considered to be: his question is simply, what was the object of the early Church's faith. It is to that question that his answer is: their faith was faith in Christ.[35] So far as it was faith *in* anything, he may well be largely right.[36] (It is interesting, however, that he should have to write a book belatedly to argue it.) To *our* question, however, he does not attend.[37]

The problem is that moderns have been so manoeuvred into defining faith in terms of its object, that we have almost lost the ability to focus on what was happening to the persons involved. To call the early Christians "believers" automatically directs our minds to something outside themselves, and diverts us from thinking that, whatever may elicit or focus it, faith may essentially be, and certainly historically was, a transforming personal experience. The New Testament text gives more emphasis to this fact than does some modern theology, or than our recent ways of conceiving religious life have allowed to come through.

If faith be primarily a quality of the person, then we err in underplaying this. Even if it be, as many would hold, a relationship—"faith is man's relation to transcendence", for example—still, both sides of the relation are involved; and "faith" is primarily the name for the human side—which alone is available for study.

(In studying Islamic religious life, I have learned that much the most fruitful approach is to pay attention to the human response. The meaning of symbols is accessible only through those for whom they are meaningful; not in themselves.)

One cannot love without loving someone. Yet the phrase "he's in love" is not too short to be eloquent. St. Paul can write, in I Corinthians 13, a hymn on love in general, and we readily follow him.

One cannot fear without being afraid of something. Yet psychiatrists speak of those who are anxiety-ridden. One does not trust if one does not trust X or Y or Z; yet there are trusting souls of whom the capacity to trust is a quality of their person.

I am insisting that faith is one of the human virtues, like courage and loyalty; and that if we are to understand human religious life we should re-learn to see it so.

Its opposite is (alas) to-day becoming more familiar, which offers a sad but important way for us to understand it better. That opposite is nihilism. If faith is insight plus commitment, lack of faith is superficiality plus *anomie*. If faith is the capacity to recognize worth and to live in terms of it, unfaith is perhaps described by the only instance where I would allow the word "believing" to be introduced: life without faith is the inability to believe in anything. If faith is confidence and trust, lack of faith is anxiety. If faith is integration of the person, is wholeness, its absence has in our secular day been given the name ego-diffusion.

Faith is a quality of human living, which at its best has taken the form of serenity and courage and service; a quiet confidence and joy that enable one to feel at home in the universe, and to find meaning in the world and in one's own life, a meaning that is profound and ultimate, and stable no matter what may happen to oneself at the level of immediate event. Men and women of this kind of faith face catastrophe or confusion, affluence or sorrow, unperturbed, face opportunity with conviction and drive, and face others with self-forgetting charity.

If, as increasingly is becoming apparent, faith be a more or less universal quality—indeed, in some ways *the* final human quality—, then it is possible to re-read the New Testament in a new light. Christ came in order that men might have faith. (He is seen then as the initiator and perfecter of our faith[38] as well as, and even for some perhaps rather than, the object of it.) Christ was important in the early Church, and the early Church was an important movement in the Mediterranean world and then in Europe, because through Christ, through the sacraments, through this movement, men and women did indeed find faith. ('Επιστευσεν [*episteusen*].)

The early Christians were unaware that other men and women in places of which they had never heard were finding faith through the Buddha, or in later centuries would find it through the Qur'an. All that they knew, and this they proclaimed, and in this they were right, was that they found it in Christ. And that news was so good that, in exultation and strength, with it they turned the world upside-down.[39] As St. Paul put it to Timothy (I:4:10): "The living God . . . is the Saviour of all men; especially of those who have faith".

Before we close this section, on what we have called the "object" of faith in Biblical usage and the absence of object, and move on to our next one, the use of our concept with an unexpressed object, we must reflect on the fact, which provides a kind of transition, that the notion of object is not in itself clear.

One may speak of the object of faith, as we have done, grammatically: the object of the verb, direct or indirect, and the like. To speak of faith's object in a logical sense, rather, has a long history: at least from the scholastics. For them, the object of the mind is truth, of the will is goodness. Moreover, each virtue has its special "object": the object of hope is always eternal beatitude;[40] the object of justice is *ius*[41] (this is so remote from modern thinking that it is almost impossible to translate this into contemporary English). In modern times the notion of object has for most persons changed drastically from this. How could it not, given the impact of the development of the distinctively modern notion of "subject", and of the massive modern notion of "objectivity", both radically new?

Perhaps it would be going too far to speculate whether, in contrast to present-day tendencies, one might in Biblical thought find a remote or partial parallel between, on the one hand, expressions like faith *in* Christ, ". . . in His name", and, on the other hand, phrases such as "joy in the Holy Spirit" (Romans 14: 17) or peace *in* Christ (John 16:33). This much, at least, one must affirm: that the word "in" (in Greek, both "in" and "into") was hardly insignificant.

St. Paul's use of the concept "in Christ" (ἐν Χριστῷ [*en Christōi*]) is particularly illustrative. He speaks in Ephesians, for instance, of persons of faith as those who were previously outside, away from, and are now inside, Christ (Ephesians 2:12-13). Certainly what has been called his "Christ-mysticism" envisages the man or woman of faith as related to the divine, including the transcendent Christ, in a union that is much less a polarized bilateral relation than is the subject/object distancing involved in many modern conceptions of human faith *vis-à-vis* an external "object". It is certainly a far cry from most modern conceptions of believing in relation to an object of believing. For St. Paul, through faith men and women are "in Christ"; and, through faith, Christ is in them.[42]

If faith is the name of a relationship between the human person and God (which has certainly been one powerful way of approximating in words to expressing its mystery), then we do well to recognize how much of an innovation it is to conceive that relation as one between a subject and an object. If one is to use theist language of this sort, then is it not better to conceive it as a relation between the two in which, rather, God is the subject? (It would be a mistake, however, to think that the human person, in turn, then becomes the object. Rather, he or she, in faith, becomes co-subject.[43])

Or, in this other pictorialization, God is locative: faith is a quality of the person or a human condition that occurs *in God*; and for Christians, in Christ.

A certain drift away from "object" terminology is, in fact, in our day discernible. Some neologisms are better than others, one may be permitted to feel. The phrase "content of faith"[44] has come into use, I believe quite recently; it disquiets me. A container is normally larger than its contents; whereas insofar as faith is a relation, it is to something or someone greater than we. Schleiermacher used, rather, *Glaubensweisen*;[45] and recently, "forms of faith" has gained ground in English. Also "shape of faith", "contours of faith", and others have appeared.[46] These show, to my mind, a welcome return to a more personalist understanding.

For Aquinas, it is important to consider that the object of faith is always God, whether one knows it or not.[47] Our apprehension of the New Testament (and for that matter of the Bhagavada Gita and of an African tribal dance) might be facilitated if—taking this Thomist cue—we discriminated clearly between the object of faith and the conscious object of faith.

V

Having moved from a propositional to a personal object, and then to no expressed object, in the Biblical presentation, there remains one more move, and then we close. It is this: to consider the unexpressed context, ideationally; the presuppositions within which the articulated conceptual expression of faith is cast; the uncriticized intellectual framework. For the first time we arrive at something to which the word "believe" might seem legitimately to apply; although after our discussion in the last chapter one may understand my malaise at using that over-worked word for this realm. We could, however, allow it in and still retain my suggestion of a new translation of the Bible quite omitting the tendentious term. The concept of believing does not occur within the Bible, even if some matters do appear there that the twentieth-century critic may accuse the Biblical writers of tacitly believing. The point is elaborate, but I shall not elaborate it. Obviously, if one thinks about it, one realizes that they believed in this sense all sorts of things that we do not; and that we believe in this sense all sorts of things that our grandchildren will not. In this sense, one might toss out an aphorism: one's faith is given by God, one's beliefs by one's century.

I make only two swift points. The first is that every comparativist has learned, and I guess that every modern man and woman is going to have to learn, to take the presuppositions of other people, other cultures, other ages, in stride. It is a mark of modern sophistication to be able to handle, without turmoil, embarrassment, or intellectual confusion, the ideational frameworks and patterns of preconceptions within which men and societies operate. This is a somewhat novel skill, but it can be learned; and in fact it is rather fun. Learning a foreign language fluently is of perhaps comparable difficulty, and comparable reward. Surely it will not be long before leaders of thought, at least, in both religious and philosophic realms, will have moved beyond that point in cultural interchange equivalent to that in language learning at which one discovers that Frenchmen are silly folk who call that object over there a *fenêtre* when in fact it is a window.

Out of Germany a while back came a movement called "demythologizing", precisely anent the New Testament, the idea being to get rid of such ideas in the Bible as appear to us now as mythological, of their time. I have long felt that on the contrary we must "remythologize", cheerily: must learn not only to recognize myths as myths but to accept them as such. A mark of having learned a foreign language reasonably well, and certainly a significant reward for having done so, is when one can read and appreciate its poetry as well as its prose.

The second point is a little more subtle. A concomitant of the first point, not needing elaborating, surely, is that one recognizes, of course, that that over there is not really a window, either. "Window" is what we call it; *fenêtre* is what the French call it; but in itself, it is neither. It is that thing, there, of which all names are but extrinsic names. Specifically, and theologically, my illustrative point is the concept of God. No Christian or Jew or other theist worth his salt but recognizes the difference between God and the concept 'God'. Certainly God is greater than my concept of Him. I know, and affirm, that He is greater than I know and affirm Him to be. Greater, and in many ways doubtless different. But that is all right. I neither disparage the concept, nor idolize it; therefore, it serves me well. (By the way, any logic that has not yet learned to deal with our knowing what transcends our knowledge, is not a logic for human persons, though it may serve for the construction of machines.)

Many have spoken of the idea of God as symbolic. I have a suggestion, which some day I may work out in detail. There seems to be merit in proposing that we think of the concept 'God' as a sacrament. As an historian, I can observe the rise of this concept in the ancient Near East, its gradual development, its special elaboration by the Jewish, then the Christian, then the Islamic movements over half the earth; its vicissitudes, its evolutions, its present-day ... shall we say, doldrums? It has been one of the most magnificent of divine-human complexes. Yet as a concept, however complex and however open to the divine, like other things human, it has been and will remain mundane and in motion. Without any question, it has been one of the most momentous of facts. To understand the idea would mean to know and to understand its role in human history.

The theists among my readers will know what I mean when I say that God has used the idea of God sacramentally as a way of entering the lives of many hundreds of millions of persons. Those who are not theists may try their hand at presuppositionalism and translate my remark into their own system—being careful that it not lose anything in the process. Personally, I find it a rich and rewarding, and reverent, suggestion. It may help some to read the Bible more understandingly, who were otherwise getting bogged down in that presuppositional-belief business. The proposal owes something to the Brahman/Isvara distinction, to the "God-beyond-God" notion, to Plotinus, as well as to Christian sacramentarianism.

VI

The task of the comparative historian of religion, in the case of any tradition or community and its faith, is first to ascertain what in fact were at any given moment and in any specific area the data of that tradition: its heritage, its institutions, its art, its rituals, its dances, its corporate structures, its doctrines. Secondly, so far as the conceptual dimension is concerned, his or her task is to uncover the tacit preconceptions, the ideational framework within which the explicit theories and formulations were embedded: what those who spoke took for granted, and what general system of meaning gave specific meaning to the particulars of all that they had to say. Thirdly, the task is to discern what all this signified to the men and women—and indeed, the children—to whom it was significant: what the symbols and notions meant, and what in the light of those symbols and notions life meant, and death, and love, and terror. He must strive to elucidate the context of persons' lives, and to discover the faith with which in that context those persons' lives were meaningfully lived. If the community concerned be a distant one, or if, as in my case in this chapter, it be one's own community in another age, the task remains at heart the same: to learn the data, and to penetrate beyond those data to the faith that they expressed and nurtured and to which they still bear witness.

Our faith must be our own; but for Christians it can be, and would do well to be, continuous with theirs, instructed and inspired by theirs. And true continuity with them will be achieved not if we reduplicate their beliefs—that would be a sorry feat, even if somehow it could be gawkily managed—but if we can emulate their faith. To that faith their beliefs, if we understand them, can guide us. Then of *our* faith, the beliefs to which we sincerely come will be the result; and if we are genuine and intelligent, the more or less adequate contemporary expression.

Within each of us, between and among all of us, within and beyond the world around us, is a reality, a truth, greater than we can grasp, but not greater than we can begin to see and to touch and to know and to respond to and to be grasped by. Certainly within each of us insofar as we are vouchsafed that quality that I am calling faith; certainly between and among us insofar as we love each other; certainly within and beyond the world around us insofar as we can relate to it well, intellectually and otherwise; is a reality, a truth, to which some people have given a name and for which some have developed an interpretation, though neither the name nor the explanation is any longer, for some, adequate to the splendour and the glory, but also to the austere . . . may we say, perhaps, terror?—certainly, the awesome majesty.

My endeavour in these lectures has not been to defend the old names or to refurbish the old interpretations; nor to propound some great new ones. My thesis is rather that the name, the interpretation, are less important than, have been and should be seen as strictly secondary to, the quality of life within us, the love between us and among us, the relation to the world. I personally am an intellectual, both by temperament and by profession. Moreover, as an historian I observe that ideas have vast consequences in human history, as do failures of ideas. It matters enormously that we find a proper belief to elucidate our faith. Part of that awesome austerity, that demand, that terror of which I speak, is the demand laid upon us to pursue the truth and to formulate it conceptually—as an inescapable obligation, yet secondary to the prior truth that precedes: the reality to which all propositions are subordinate.

Notes and References
Indexes

Notes and References

Chapter I

1. Arthur Darby Nock. Professor Nock, whom I had known personally somewhat, died shortly before I took up my appointment at Harvard; this remark I did not hear directly from him. It was among the rich lore that I found that he had bequeathed. Although not more fully documentable, it is beautifully in character: it rings authentic.

2. This is not to be written off as merely "disciplinary" specialization. The attempt to understand the rich religious history of, for instance, India is immensely rewarding but sufficiently difficult that one looks for help wherever one may find it; and find it one does from sociologists and anthropologists, psychiatrists, economic historians, phenomenologists, existentialists, metaphysicians, archaeologists, philologists, numismatists, and many another.

3. Much recent anti-religious philosophy of religion seems to display an animus, and to be motivated by a deliberate seeking to depreciate. Although this seems evident on reading, one would be hesitant to make such a charge against presumably serious scholars. Yet Nielsen virtually admits it explicitly (though presumably inadvertently). He says in so many words that the critical analysts were engaged in an "attempt [sic] to find a general meaning criterion in virtue of which the putative truth-claims of religion can be shown to be unintelligible or incoherent"; and when this failed they have worked "instead . . . in an attempt [sic] to establish [sic] the actual incoherence or at least the baselessness" of such "claims". He says this with reference to Findlay, Edwards, Farrell, Hepburn, Martin, Matson, Flew, and himself. Kai Nielsen, *Contemporary Critiques of Religion*, London: Macmillan, 1971 (John Hick, ed., Philosophy of Religion Series), p. 114.

4. *Mahāvākya* (Sanskrit; literally, "great saying"): one of certain pronouncements from the Upaniṣads that the Hindu tradition has regarded as of transcending import. Often twelve are listed; they include "That thou art" (*tat tvam asi*), "I am Brahman" (*aham brahmāsmi*), *ātman* is *Brahman*, etc.

5. Arthur Waley's translation, in his *Three Ways of Thought in Ancient China*, London: Allen & Unwin, 1939, p. 79.

6. *Chung Yung*, chap. 12: adapted from Lin Yutang's version of the translation of Ku Hungming, in Lin Yutang, ed. and trans., *The Wisdom of Confucius*, New York: Random House, Modern Library, 1938, p. 108 (cf. p. 102).

7. A. J. Ayer, *The Central Questions of Philosophy*, London: Weidenfeld and Nicolson, 1973.

8. For an impressive depiction pictorially of the cow of heaven on the tomb of the pharaoh Sethi I at Thebes, from a drawing by Howard Carter, see *The Journal of Egyptian Archaeology*, vol. 28 (1942), plate IV (opposite p. 38). For a verbal presentation, cf. Henri Frankfort, *Kingship and the Gods: A Study of Ancient Near Eastern Religion as the Integration of Society & Nature*, Chicago & London: University of Chicago Press [1948], 1965: "the sky . . . is a cow" (p. 156); "the sky is a huge cow" (p. 162). For some interpretive elaborations, cf. ref. 12 below. (Note: Here and throughout these notes I indicate, of course, in each case the edition used by me but specify

also, for historical purposes, the original publication of the works cited, giving in brackets the date, and on occasion other data, in cases where I have not myself seen a copy of that original—or in some instances, usually of recent works, may have seen it but prefer to use a subsequent, sometimes author-revised, edition.)

9. Hat-hor (Ḥwt Ḥr); also, at times, Nut and others.

10. The interpretations, following Herder and von Humboldt, developed by the anthropologist Sapir and more especially by his student Whorf. See David G. Mandelbaum, ed., *Selected Writings of Edward Sapir in Language, Culture and Personality,* Berkeley and Los Angeles: University of California Press, and London: Cambridge University Press [1949], 1958, and John B. Carroll, ed., *Language, Thought, and Reality: Selected Writings of Benjamin Lee Whorf,* Cambridge, Mass.: Massachusetts Institute of Technology [1956], paperback reprint 1966. Edward Sapir, *Language: An Introduction to the Study of Speech,* New York: Harcourt, Brace, 1921 takes on the whole a somewhat different view.

11. Buber's *I-Thou* in general, and in particular his enunciating, for instance, of his perceiving a tree as "thou", should help any modern thinker towards an openness, at least, to the ancient Egyptians' orientation. See Martin Buber, *Ich und Du.* This was first published Leipzig: Insel [1923]. A "Nachwort", dated 1957, was published in the new edition of the work, Heidelberg: Lambert Schneider [1958]. I have used the German text in Martin Buber, *Werke,* München: Kösel, and Heidelberg: Lambert Schneider, Bd. I, 1962, pp. 77-170. The discussion on the tree is found pp. 81-82 (*Nachwort,* § 2, pp. 161-63). In the two English translations, this passage appears as follows: *I and Thou,* Ronald Gregor Smith, trans. [Edinburgh: T. & T. Clark, 1937], 2nd edn., New York: Scribner's, 1958, pp. 7-8, 124-26; Walter Kaufmann, trans., New York: Scribner's, 1970, pp. 57-59, 172-73.

12. For interpretive expositions, see H. Frankfort, *Ancient Egyptian Religion: An Interpretation* [New York, Columbia University Press, 1948], Harper Torchbook, the Cloister Library, New York: Harper & Row, 1961, pp. 15, 19, and esp. the same author's *Kingship* (our ref. 8 above), chap. 14, "The Power in Cattle: Procreation", pp. 162-80, particularly "B. Sun and Sky", pp. 168-71. Otherwise, the literature of modern scholarship on ancient Egyptian religion in general is, of course, immense; I have read in it in somewhat desultory fashion. Among many others I have found helpful in general Étienne Drioton et Jacques Vandier, *L'Égypte,* 4ᵉ édn., Paris: Presses Universitaires de France, 1962 (Clio: Introduction aux études historiques: Les peuples de l'orient méditerranéen, II), esp. chap. 3, "La Religion" (pp. 61-128), and Jacques Vandier, *La Religion égyptienne,* Paris: Presses Universitaires de France, 1949 (Mana: Introduction à l'histore des religions, I: Les anciennes religions orientales, I). These, however, and other more recent works such as Siegfried Morenz, *Ägyptische Religion,* Stuttgart: Kohlhammer (Christel Matthias Schröder, ed., *Die Religionen der Menschheit,* Bd. 8), 1960 (*Egyptian Religion,* Ann E. Keep, trans., London: Methuen, and Ithaca, N.Y.: Cornell, 1973) illuminate our particular problem only indirectly. Despite the title, this is even more true of G. A. Wainwright, *The Sky-Religion in Egypt* [Cambridge, England: Cambridge University Press, 1938], Westport, Conn.: Greenwood, 1971.

13. For example: E. E. Evans-Pritchard, *Nuer Religion,* Oxford: Clarendon, 1956, especially chapter x, "The Sacrificial Role of Cattle", pp. 248 ff., and Godfrey Lienhardt, *Divinity and Experience: The Religion of the Dinka,* Oxford: Clarendon, 1961, especially Introduction, § (ii), pp. 10-27, "Cattle in Dinka Thought" (so the Table of Contents; the heading on p. 10 reads rather, "Cattle in Dinka Experience"). These speak of a religious perception of cattle, but virtually without mention of any celestial dimension;

the one instance of reference to the sky would seem to be in a hymn cited by Evans-Pritchard, p. 99. Similarly the earlier substantial study of Melville J. Herskovits, "The Cattle Complex in East Africa", indicates only terrestrial concerns (*American Anthropologist,* 28 [new series] : 230-72, 361-88, 494-528, 633-64 [1926]. I have seen the New York: Kraus, 1962 reprint). These help one to apprehend, perhaps, the cow part, if not the sky part, of the ancient Egyptian perception.

14. In oral and private communications from Dr. Jeffery Hopkins of the University of Virginia, as to Tibetan extrapolations of the better-known Indian *kāmadhenu* ("cow of plenty") notion. (On this last, see s.v. in the Sanskrit dictionaries; also s.vv. *kāmadugha, kāmaduh,* etc.; and the commentaries on Bhagavad Gitā 3:10. See also Benjamin Walker, *Hindu World: An Encyclopedic Survey of Hinduism,* London: Allen & Unwin, 2 voll., 1968, I. 515-16).

15. Nielsen, *Critiques* (our ref. 3 above), p. 115.

16. Ibid.

17. Or, for philosophers to persuade anyone to disbelieve it.

18. A practice has developed among linguistic philosophers of discriminating between "statements" and "propositions", of which the former may be recognized as historical, culture-specific, and personalist. If propositions be thought of as not so, however, then they become metaphysical; yet linguistic analysts tend to be unsatisfactory metaphysicians. I find of passing interest, for instance, Ryle's paper "Are There Propositions?" first presented early in 1930 before the Aristotelian Society, London, published in that society's Proceedings, 30: [91]-126 (1930), and reprinted in Gilbert Ryle, *Collected Papers,* London: Hutchinson, 2 voll., 1971, II. 12-38.

19. In the Cadbury Lectures delivered at the University of Birmingham, England, 1972; to be published in due course in a volume tentatively entitled "Towards a Theology of Comparative Religion".

20. This position seems perhaps to have been first bluntly stated in A. J. Ayer, *Language, Truth and Logic* [London: Gollancz, 1936]. I have used the Pelican edition, Harmondsworth: Penguin, 1974, where the passage in question is pp. 152-53. In his more recent writing—for instance, his Gifford Lectures (above, ref. 7)—he moderates this position somewhat, but does not fundamentally change it. Others have seemed to follow his earlier position at times without moderation.

Chapter II

1. Tentatively entitled *Faith & Belief.*

2. Wilfred Cantwell Smith, *The Meaning and End of Religion: A New Approach to the Religious Traditions of Mankind,* New York: Macmillan, 1963. See chap. 7, "Faith" (pp. 170-92). Specifically on "the expression of faith in the form of belief" (p. 172), see § vi, pp. 180-85. In the paperback edition (New York: New American Library, Mentor Books, 1964), these references are: pp. 154-73, 155, 162-67.

3. In my forthcoming *Faith & Belief,* see chap. 5,"*Credo* and Roman Catholic views on faith", where the material on which this paragraph rests is presented and analysed at length.

4. This is the standard etymology, rather well established. Recently part of it has been challenged; I have in mind to publish presently an article defending a modified version of it against the new criticisms, which I find in significant part unpersuasive, and

which in any case do not affect our argument here. There is a technical discussion in my *Faith & Belief*, chap. 4, ref. 35.

5. *Faith & Belief*, chap. 6: "The English word *believe*", where the material on which the present couple of paragraphs rest is presented and analysed at length, and where the material presented and analysed in the remainder of this present chapter is briefly summarized.

6. One example: of five manuscripts of the fourteenth-century Scottish poem "The Pistill of Susan" (sc., The Epistle of Susan: a versified re-telling of the apocryphal Biblical story "Susanna and the Elders"), the five versions of lines 164-65 read as follows (the meaning is that they sware by the Lord and the law that they held dear):

> Bi þe lord and þe lawe þat we onne leeue."
> Þey swere;
>
> Bi þe lord *and* þe lawe þat we on leeue."
> Þei swere;
>
> By þat lord *and* þe lawe þat we on leve."
> They swere;
>
> Be þe lorde *and* þe lay þat we apon leue
> In fere."
>
> Be þat lorde *and* þe lawe þat we on be-leue."
> They swere;

And of line 358, as follows (he that loves that Lord, there is no need for him to get lost):

> Hose leeueþ on þat lord, þar him not lees
> Ho so leeueþ on þat lord, þar hym not lees
> Who so leviþ on our lord dar hym not lese
> Now qwo so loues oure lorde wele, thare him neuer lese
> He þat loueth þat lorde, þar hym not drede, no lees

See F. J. Amours, ed., *Scottish Alliterative Poems in Riming Stanzas* [Edinburgh: the Scottish Text Society, 1897], New York and London: Johnson reprint, 1966, pp. 179, 214-15, 187, 244-45.

For other instances of this type, as well as a much more elaborate setting forth of the whole mediaeval development of this term and concept in English, see my *Faith & Belief*, chap 6.

7. The Second Nun's Tale; preliminary Invocation, line 63. Walter W. Skeat, ed., *The Complete Works of Geoffrey Chaucer*, vol. IV, *The Canterbury Tales: Text*, Oxford: Clarendon, 1894, p. 511.

8. *Faith & Belief*, chap. 3: "The Islamic Instance".

9. Statistics here and throughout this study are calculated, for the 1611 version, from Robert Young, *Analytical Concordance to the Bible* [Edinburgh, 1879], 22nd American edn., rev., Grand Rapids, Mich.: Eerdmans, 1973.

10. For these and subsequent Shakespeare statistics, I have relied on Marvin Spevack, *A Complete and Systematic Concordance to the Works of Shakespeare*, 6 voll., Hildesheim: Georg Olms, 1968-70. In the figure for "faith", I have included the seven instances of his use of the plural "faiths", but not his singleton participle "faith'd". My figures are based on the entries in vol. 4; the statement here given about the verb (total occurrences in all forms: 290) is based on the "Word-Frequency Index" constituting Appendix A of vol. 6 (pp. 4177 ff.).

11. Francis Lord Verulam, Viscount St. Alban, *Sylva Sylvarum: or, a Natural History* [published after the author's death by William Rawley, London: William Lee, 1627], § 947. I have used the edition of James Spedding et al., edd., *The Works of Francis Bacon* . . . [London, 1857-74], new edn., 14 voll., London: Longmans et al., 1868-92, where this occurs twice on II. 656. He also speaks here of "belief in an art", as constituting along with "belief in a man" two types of belief on authority, but the latter type is "far the more active"; he further notes that belief on authority is "far the most potent" form of what he calls belief, since other forms "will stagger" (§ 946; same page). For his use of "belief" of a person's word, cf. ref. 19 below. In that case also, as we shall there note, the acceptance involved is expressly of the person who speaks. Although I have by no means made a thorough and systematic study, my impression is that the noun "belief", and especially the verb "to believe", are relatively rare in Bacon's English style, and that "believe that . . ." is particularly so; but I may be wrong in this. At least in 1605, it would seem that outside of discussion of religious matters, he tended in cases where we to-day might use the words "belief" and "believe", to employ rather "opinion". In the *Advancement of Learning*, I note that he seems to use the word "opinion", and not "belief": (cf. "I am of opinion that . . ." II. xi. 1), especially when speaking of the philosophers: of Aristotle (II. vii. 2); "the opinion of Plato" (II. ix. 3); the Skeptics and Academics "held opinion that . . ." (II. xiii. 4); of the later Academy and Cicero, "this opinion" (II. xiii. 4); "the opinion of Socrates" (II. xxi. 4); "The opinion of Aristotle" (II. xxii. 8); etc. (These instances are culled from a cursory survey. *Thee Twoo Bookes of Francis Bacon, of the Proficience and Advancement of Learning, Divine and Humane* [London: Henrie Tomes, 1605]. In The World's Classics edition, with a preface by Thomas Case, *Bacon's Advancement of Learning* . . ., London: Oxford University Press [1906], 1929, pp. 127, 100, 117, 135, 136, 172, 184 respectively.)

12. Thomas Hobbes of Malmesbury, *Leviathan; or the Matter, Forme, and Power of a Common-wealth Ecclesiasticall and Civil* [London: Andrew Crooke, 1651], Part I, chap. vii. In the "Pelican Classics" edn., C. B. Macpherson, ed., Harmondsworth: Penguin Books [1968], 1972, p. 132. The original is in italics.

13. Ibid., III. xliii (p. 612).

14. Ibid., III. xliii (p. 612)

15. Ibid., I. vii (pp. 132-33). The original is in italics.

16. Ibid., I. vii (p. 133).

17. One example from among several: ibid., III. xliii (p. 615).

18. Ibid., I. vii (p. 133).

19. For example, in the culminating chapter of his *Advancement of Learning*. In the Spedding edn., III. 477 ff.; in the Case edn., pp. 221 ff: esp. the first two paragraphs of chap. xxv, from which all the citations here are taken. In this passage he speaks of believing God's word, and makes it evident that the point of this lies in its being His: that is, it lies in or is constituted by an allegiance to or trust of Him, and explicitly not in an act of the reason operating on the propositional content of that word. Otherwise—if we

were to "believe" only what is independently persuasive—"we give consent to the matter, and not to the author"(the comma is found in the Case edn., p. 221, not in the Spedding edn., III. 478); and that is quite another affair. Furthermore, belief is expressly here a matter of interpersonal relation. "In belief it" [sc. "man's mind"—preceding clause] "suffereth from [in modern English: is acted upon by] spirit"—not, as it does in knowledge, "from sense" (same page). Also, "belief" and "faith" are here used, evidently, interchangeably: each of these two paragraphs begins with the former word and ends with the latter. Moreover, the relation of person to person constituted here on earth by belief or faith will become in Heaven a knowledge that is similarly interpersonal: "faith shall cease, and we shall know as we are known" (same page). In the version of this work subsequently published in Latin (other hands effected this, but "Bacon took a great deal of pains with it himself . . . so that we must consider the whole translation as stamped with his authority"—Spedding, I. 420), "belief" is rendered as *fides*; also, the sentence above where the English reads that in belief "it suffereth from spirit" is made more explicitly personalist in that while "man's mind" in the preceding clause is duly rendered as *mens humana*, "it" in the second clause is explicated *in fide autem anima patitur ab anima*. Francisci Baronis de Verulamio . . . *De Dignitate et Augmentis Scientiarum* libri ix [Londini: Joannis Haviland, 1623]. Spedding edn., I. 830.

20. Hobbes, *Leviathan*, I. vii (p. 133).

21. He never uses "belief" as synonymous with "opinion", it seems; but sometimes he differentiates between them as two distinct matters, while at other times (cf. our next ref. just below) he calls "belief" one particular type of opinion. To use more recent phrasing: for him, faith is not belief *simpliciter*; it is either different from it, or is belief of a special sort. In either case, the distinction is for him on the ground that what he calls "beleefe" involves and rests upon an interpersonal relationship. Thus in *Leviathan*, I. vii, he writes: ". . . it beginneth either at some . . . contemplation of his own, and then it is . . . called Opinion; Or it beginneth at some saying of another, . . . and then . . . is called BELEEFE, and FAITH". In this case he remarks, "the Discourse is not so much concerning the Thing, as the Person". (Furthermore, the two matters—on the one hand, "opinion"; on the other, "beleef" or "faith" or "trust"— are not quite of the same order, in that he calls the former "discourse" and the latter [its?] "resolution".) (All these citations: Macpherson edn., p. 132.)

22. "Belief defined. And particularly, when the opinion is admitted out of trust to other men, they are said to believe it; and their admittance of it is called belief, and sometimes faith. . . . Belief . . . is the admitting of propositions upon trust". Thomas Hobbes, *Human Nature, or the Fundamental Elements of Policy: Being a Discovery of the Faculties, Acts, and Passions, of the Soul of Man, from Their Original Causes, as Are Not Commonly Known or Asserted*, London [1640], chap. vi, § § 7, 9. I have used the edition in Sir William Molesworth, ed., *The English Works of Thomas Hobbes of Malmesbury*, London: John Bohn, 11 voll., 1839-45; this passage is IV. 29-30. I have omitted the original's italics.

23. Hobbes, *Leviathan*, I. vii (p. 132). (Italics omitted.)

24. Hobbes, *Human Nature;* see our ref. 22 just above.

25. Hobbes, *Leviathan*, III. xliii (p. 612).

26. [John Locke,] *An Essay concerning Humane Understanding*, London [Thomas Bassett, 1690], IV. xviii. 2. In the edition of Alexander Campbell Fraser, 2 voll., Oxford: Clarendon, 1894, this is II. 416. In the abridged edition of A. S. Pringle-Pattison, Oxford: Clarendon [1924], 1969, p. 355. Both editors have modernized spelling.

27. Locke, *Essay*, IV. xv. 3. Fraser edn., II. 365; cf. P.-P., p. 335.

28. Two instances may illustrate this. One is *Essay,* I. iii. 24; Fraser, I. 115. In Pringle-Pattison, this is given as I. iv. 24, p. 40. In this case, Locke seems spontaneously to combine the notions of believing and trusting a person, as follows: "What he believes only, and takes upon trust . . ." (cf. his next paragraph: ". . . believing and taking . . . upon trust"–I. iii/iv. 25: p. 116/41). The other example is from IV. xv. 5 (Fraser, II. 367; cf. P.-P., p. 336): [in certain circumstances] ". . . the most untainted credit of a witness will scarce be able to find belief. As it happened to a Dutch ambassador, who entertaining the king of Siam with the particularities of Holland, which he was inquisitive after, amongst other things told him, that the water in his country would sometimes, in cold weather, be so hard, that men walked upon it, and that it would bear an elephant, if he were there. To which the king replied, Hitherto I have believed the strange things you have told me, because I look upon you as a sober fair man, but now I am sure you lie". In this passage, and the sentences that precede it, it is explicitly a matter of "testimony" and the "credit" (from Latin *credo*: the mediaeval word for personal faith) of a person. (In the Pringle-Pattison edition, the text varies insignificantly. I have omitted italics.)

29. John Stuart Mill, *A System of Logic, Ratiocinative and Inductive, Being a Connected View of the Principles of Evidence, and the Methods of Scientific Investigation,* 2 voll., London: Parker, 1843, chap. 1, § 2 (vol. I, p. 22). (Italics original.)

30. *Chambers's Encyclopædia: New Edition,* London: George Newnes, 1959, entry "Belief". Two of these three statements are somewhat qualified, in that the first is introduced with the words: "Indeed it would seem to be clear that . . . what we actually believe, in strictness of language, is always . . ."; and the third, with the words "The answer would seem to be that . . ."—although in this last case the "would seem to be" perhaps qualifies not the proposition that follows but the view that that proposition answers a query that has been raised.

31. In the second sector of these creeds ("I believe in Jesus Christ . . ."), subordinate clauses qualifying in a descriptive way the Second Person of the Trinity are, in the official Latin translation and most English ones, cast in the form of relative clauses that include finite verbs (*qui conceptus est* . . . , "who was conceived by the Holy Ghost . . ." etc.), although in strict logic these qualifying clauses are not propositions. In the original Greek, there are no finite verbs, all such descriptive qualifications taking the form rather of participles. For the Greek and Latin texts, I have used the versions as given in William A. Curtis, *A History of Creeds and Confessions of Faith in Christendom and Beyond, with Historical Tables,* Edinburgh: T. & T. Clark, 1911, pp. 64, 74-75. A few propositions (fewer than one might imagine) are to be found in the "Confession of our Christian fayth" known as *Quicunque vult,* and sometimes, erroneously, as "The Athanasian Creed" (neither, as has been remarked, is it rightly attributed to St. Athanasius, nor is it strictly a creed). The word "beleue" is used three times in the English translation of this included in the 1549 Book of Common Prayer of the Church of England (pp. 31-33). Once the verb is followed by a direct single object ("beleue faythfully [the Catholyke fayth]"—originally, perhaps, "to hold dear"; or, in the words of the confession itself, to "kepe holy and undefyled" and to "holde"). Once it occurs with an indirect single object ("beleue ryghtly in the incarnacion of oure Lorde Jesu Christe"). Once the use, though slightly ambiguous, is presumably with a propositional object: ". . . the ryght fayth is that we beleue and confesse: that our Lorde Jesu Christe the sonne of God, is God and manne" (—here "beleue" is presumably correlate with "confesse" so that the "that" clause that follows is the object of both verbs). I should imagine that the use of this statement in the church services of the Anglican Church played a significant role in the developments of English-speaking Christians' changing

notions of what "believing" signifies; it was the focus of controversy in the nineteenth century, for instance. *The First Prayer Book of King Edward VI*, London: Moring, De La More Press, 1903 (Vernon Staley, ed., The Library of Liturgiology & Ecclesiology for English Readers, vol. II). In averring that the main creeds contained no propositions, I am, of course, taking the principal verb clauses, "I believe . . ." not as propositions but as performatives; cf. our next ref. just below.

32. An exposition of the early significance of the rite of baptism, as the original occasion for the use and development of creeds as performatives, is given in chap. 5 of my forthcoming *Faith & Belief*, along with some bibliography of others' studies of the matter.

33. In the plays, "believing that" is common; but it is less common than believing a person, and substantially less frequent than the combined instances of believing a person, a thing, or a person's word. With the noun, only 2 out of 15 occurrences are "belief that". J. Spevack, *Concordance*, s.vv.

34. *A New English Dictionary on Historical Principles* . . . , James A. H. Murray, ed., vol. I, Oxford: Clarendon, and New York: Macmillan, 1888, s.v. "Belief". The whole article is, of course, fascinating and important.

35. *Webster's Third New International Dictionary of the English Language, Unabridged*, Philip Babcock Gove, ed., Springfield, Mass.: Merriam, 1961. *The American Heritage Dictionary of the English Language*, William Morris, ed., Boston, New York, etc.: American Heritage, Houghton Mifflin, 1969. *The Random House Dictionary of the English Language*, Jess Stein, ed., New York: Random House, 1966.

36. Mill, *Logic*, vol. I, p. 21. The words "express themselves" here are not insignificant; similarly, earlier in the same paragraph, he wrote: "Whatever can be an object of belief, or even of disbelief, must, *when put into words*, assume the form of a proposition" (I. 21) —emphasis mine. Such qualifications as these presently got lost by the wayside. Mill's use of them indicates that he is still at the beginning of the new phase. Yet the very next sentence to the statement just quoted is, without any such qualification, the dictum cited below, at our reference 38. There were precedents for the view that Mill here sets forward: he was formalizing and emphasizing one strand in the tradition that he inherited. Hobbes, for instance, had said, although I get the impression that this is very much in passing, "*truth, and a true proposition*, is all one" (*Human Nature*, V, § 10; Molesworth edn., IV. 24); and Locke, in a chapter that he explicitly entitles "Of True and False Ideas" (*Essay*, II. xxxii—Fraser I. 514-26; P.-P., pp. 215 f.), nevertheless remarks in its opening sentence that in a stricter use of language "truth and falsehood belong . . . only to propositions" (§ 1—Fraser, I. 514), not to ideas; yet by the end of the discussion he has modified this to say more cautiously that, rather, truth and falsehood "will, I think [*sic*], scarce [*sic*] agree to them" (sc. to ideas, except insofar as they contain propositions) (§ 26; p. 525), and he allows, in passing, that there is also "a metaphysical sense of the word truth" (§ 2—Fraser, I. 514). Later he writes, more firmly, "truth properly belongs only to propositions" (IV. v. 2—Fraser, II. 244; P.-P., p. 290). Looking further back, one may of course say that Mill was developing the Aristotelian, as distinct from the Platonic, strand in Western thought—but developing it far beyond anything that can be blamed on Aristotle! (Aristotle's definition of truth and falsity is not of what is said, but the saying of it. *Metaphysics* IV. vii. 1011b. 25-29. The Jaeger edn., Oxford: Clarendon, 1957, p. 83.)

37. Ayer, *Central Questions* (above, our chap. I, ref. 7), p. 211.

38. Mill, *Logic*, vol. I, p. 21.

39. Cf. Wilfred Cantwell Smith, "A Human View of Truth". This was first delivered as a lecture at a conference on the philosophy of religion at the University of Birmingham, England, 1970. It is published in the proceedings of that conference: John Hick, ed., *Truth and Dialogue: The Relationship between World Religions,* London: Sheldon, 1974; *Truth and Dialogue in World Religions: Conflicting Truth-Claims*, Philadelphia: Westminster, n.d., pp. [20]-44 (also: "Conflicting Truth-Claims: A Rejoinder", pp.[156]-162). The paper was published also in *SR: Studies in Religion / Sciences religieuses*, Toronto, 1:[6]-24 (1971). Among other matters, this presentation considers a world-view (in this case, the Islamic) where another view of truth than the propositional has obtained.

40. So far as the participle ("believing") is concerned, I have counted its agreeing with "I" and "me", or with "he / she", "it", etc.

41. See his discussions of (sc. our) human believing in general, especially his sections "Of the nature of the idea or belief" and "Of the causes of belief", in his *Human Nature* (Book I, Part III, § § vii, viii) and his second thoughts on these particular matters a year later (published as an Appendix to the third volume, 1740). The presentation is virtually throughout in the first person, whether singular or plural. An example, from the opening paragraph: "We conceive many things, which we do not believe. In order then to discover more fully the nature of belief, or the qualities of those ideas we assent to, let us . . . ." Again: "propositions, to which I do not assent . . . I clearly understand". It may be noted also that not only the first-person form of the verb is regularly used but also on occasion quite casually the second, although this is rarer. An example: he illustrates his notions by considering in passing the case of ". . . a person, who does not assent to a proposition you advance". David Hume, *A Treatise of Human Nature: Being an Attempt to Introduce the Experimental Method of Reasoning into Moral Subjects*, London: John Noon, 3 voll. [1739-40]. I have used the edition by L. A. Selby-Bigge, Oxford: Clarendon [1888], 1973, where these passages are found as follows: pp. 94-106, [623]-639; 94, 95, 95. For further examples, cf. our reff. 73, 75 below. This matter is intertwined with the question of the truth of what is believed, and is accordingly elaborated there a little under that heading. Cf. also the Selby-Bigge index, s.v. "Belief", pp. 644-45.

42. Somewhat less colloquially: "You'd better believe". For both, with dated early examples, see William Craigie et al., *A Dictionary of American English on Historical Principles,* 4 voll., Chicago: University of Chicago Press, 1936-44, s.v. "Better". In 1974, Eastern Airlines, I noticed, spent some part of their advertising budget confronting the Boston public with large billboards reading "Daily flights to Miami? You gotta believe!". What the company officials thought that these words meant is perhaps not a valid question, but the move would seem to suggest that they or their advertising agency supposed that among the populace at large the phrasing would stir some sense perhaps as much moral still as propositional—having to do with what is good, and with action, as much as with what is true?

43. Language philosophers are beginning to notice, I gather, a number of "paradoxes" emerging when they attend to discourse in the first person singular. Their logic, geared for scientific observational reports and for machines, creaks when fed more personalist phrasings. These problems do not arise for those of us for whom of truth and rationality the scientific is one sub-field only, and in whose view the locus of meaning is persons, their language thus subordinate to them.

44. Donald D. Evans, *The Logic of Self-Involvement: A Philosophical Study of Everyday Language with Special Reference to the Christian Use of Language of God as Creator,* London: SCM, 1963.

45. ". . . so muss ich nicht einmal sagen: *es ist* moralisch gewiss, dass ein Gott sei usw., sondern: *ich bin* moralisch gewiss usw.*" (Emphasis original.) Immanuel Kant, *Critik der reinen Vernunft* [Riga: Hartknoch, 1781; 2nd edn., *Kritik . . .,* 1787], II. 2. 3 (B 857; cf. A 829). I have used the Leipzig: Insel, 1922 edition (vol. 3 of the *Sämtliche Werke*). where this passage is p. 624. Cf. Norman Kemp Smith, trans., *Immanuel Kant's Critique of Pure Reason,* London: Macmillan [1929], 1950, p. 650. It may be remarked that in this section Kant manifestly is taking not yet an impersonally propositional view of knowing and of *glauben,* but a view of these as a personal judgement (*Urteil*), and is holding (wrongly? atypically? unlike Luther) that believing in God means believing that He exists. (Cf. *Das Fürwahrhalten* in the opening sentence of this section, B 848 [cf. A 820] and note the definition of *Glauben,* B 850 [cf. A 822], pp. 617, 619; English, pp. 645, 646. Cf. also B 854 [A 826]: "die Lehre vom Dasein Gottes zum doktrinalen Glauben gehöre"–p. 621; Eng., p. 648.) More historically, we should phrase this that at the end of the eighteenth century he was writing at a time when the German *glauben* had come to mean this for many persons, including him. Refinements, however, are in order. In addition to his recognizing that its meaning is of the first person singular, not of the third (we may say, rather: for him, this was still evident), two further points illuminate the stage at which he is to be located in the modern development of the meaning of our term. First, while he equates it with *fürwahrhalten,* "holding to be true", nonetheless he states explicitly that *glauben* is a term that may be used with regard to making a judgement only in cases where there is a practical dimension, involving the one who so judges in acting, or at least in a readiness to act. Even when the judgement might seem to be purely theoretical (is theoretical, we might say, in the Aristotelian sense that its object is not subject to change by one's acting), it can be termed *Glauben* only by analogy ("so gibt es in bloss theoretischen Urteilen ein *Analogon* von *praktischen"*: B 853 [cf. A 825], p. 621; English, p. 648; emphasis original]. This–he calls it *doktrinale Glauben,* in distinction from his more formally practical other kinds, *pragmatische Glauben* and *moralische Glauben* (pp. 621, 620, 623) –can be termed *Glauben* in that, he says, in this case also there is added, as in the others, a readiness to follow through in practice (as, explicitly, in betting) by a staking of one's possessions, little or much, and eventually one's life, on the judgement. That is, like many modern Christians still to-day, Kant has moved towards into the phase where *glauben* and "believing" name the holding of an opinion, and yet he lives still also in that phase when it meant "holding dear", and therefore adds this to the other (more accurately: adds the other to this). (See our next section for a discussion of this development in English.) Secondly, among human judgements he discriminates also those for the truth of which the grounds are seen to be adequate both objectively and subjectively, those for which they are so subjectively but not objectively, and those that are seen to be inadequate on both counts. The first of these classes we call "knowing", and he called it *Wissen.* The third in twentieth-century English is called "believing"; he called it *Meinen.* (Norman Kemp Smith translates this as "opining".) Kant reserved the word *Glauben* for a judgement that the person who holds it has not "persuasion" (*Überredung*) but full certainty as to its truth. We might say: he lived at a stage when it was still theoretically and practically possible for the term to designate this middle class of judgements. He did *not* mean a judgement of the third class that the person holding it *thinks* to be certain–a non-rational opinion held with force (vehemence: "blind faith"). See the section *Vom Meinen, Wissen und Glauben* (pp. 617-25; in English, "Opining, Knowing, and Believing" [so Kemp Smith; one might suggest, "Believing, Knowing, Faith", but the ambiguity is inherent, given the date at which he was writing] , pp. 645-52; B 848-59; cf. A 820-31).

The best way to read this entire section, I suggest, is to do so historically: to understand him as transitional between an earlier era in which *credo* and its vernacular counterparts had named a moral act (pledging allegiance to what was culturally and individually recognized as obtaining) and a later one in which "believing" or *Glauben* now names the holding of an opinion. Read thus, each of his points in the section falls readily into place. Nonetheless, in general I leave to others an exploration of the exact historical evolution of the meanings of *glauben* in German and of *croire* in French; I am not in a position to document or to refute my first impression that over the centuries these have roughly paralleled the development that I have surprised myself by finding for "believe" in English, nor my guess that German has moved somewhat more slowly than the other two.

46. Except in the past tense. This exception has become religiously crucial.

47. This was reprinted in 1973 from earlier versions of the Fourteenth Edition; I have traced it no further back than the 1962 impression, but how much prior to that it be I do not know. Both the similarities and the differences between this and the much abbreviated 1974 Britannica Micropaedia article are engaging.

48. I owe this observation to my colleague at Dalhousie University, F. Hilton Page, who in connection with it draws my attention to the remark of Mavrodes in George I. Mavrodes, ed., *The Rationality of Belief in God,* Englewood Cliffs, N.J.: Prentice-Hall, 1970, p. 17. Pertinent also, I might suggest, is a point made by Jaspers in the course of his consideration of what is common, and what different, among his four "standard-setting" (*massgebende*) figures, Socrates, the Buddha, K'ung Fu-tzu, and Jesus Christ: namely, that all these "know silence and accentuate it. . . . of their deepest truth partaking is possible only indirectly, even for themselves", and that none of them set down what he had to teach in written form (*Die vier kennen und betonen das Schweigen. . . . ihre tiefste Wahrheit kann nur indirekt mitteilbar werden, auch für sie selber. . . . Sie haben keine Werke geschrieben*). Karl Jaspers, *Die grossen Philosophen,* vol. I, München : R. Piper, 1957, pp. 225, 226. (Translation mine. A variant wording is available in the version of Hannah Arendt, ed., Ralph Manheim, trans.: Karl Jaspers, *The Great Philosophers: The Foundations* and Karl Jaspers, *Socrates, Buddha, Confucius, Jesus: The Paradigmatic Individuals,* both New York: Harcourt, Brace & World, 1962, pp. 104 and 94 respectively.)

49. More fully: "The basic form of faith is indicated in the statements: I believe you; I believe in you. To believe some*thing* is but a secondary form of this". Heinrich Fries, "Faith and Knowledge" in *Sacramentum Mundi: An Encyclopedia of Theology,* Karl Rahner et al., edd., Freiburg: Herder, Bruges: Desclée de Brouwer, New York: Herder and Herder, London: Burns & Oates, Montreal: Palm, etc., 6 voll., 1968-70.

50. The full passage reads as follows: ". . . truth, which only doth judge itself, teacheth, that the inquiry of truth, which is the love-making, or wooing of it, the knowledge of truth, which is the presence of it, and the belief of truth, which is the enjoying of it, is the sovereign good of human nature". (The final "is" here either is to be understood as "are", inquiry, knowledge, and belief constituting a compound subject, or else these three are the predicate, the subject of "is" being the last six words of the sentence. Bacon's *Essays* were first published in 1597, with subsequent editions in 1606, 1612, 1613; but this particular essay appeared first in the edition of 1625, where it constitutes the first. I have used the following edition: *The Works of Francis Bacon, Lord Chancellor of England. A New Edition: with a Life of the Author,* by Basil Montagu. Philadelphia: Hart, 3 voll., 1853, where the brief essay is found in full on I. 11.

51. See the present writer, "Faith as *Taṣdīq*" in Parwez Morewedge, ed., *Studies in Islamic Philosophy & Science,* Albany: State University of New York Press, forthcoming.

52. This is not unrelated to the fact of the first- and second-person subject. A contention, it has struck me, might be raised that to use Shakespeare's plays to illustrate the thesis of personalism, through the verbal forms, and the concomitant thesis here of truth-relatedness, perhaps begs the question somewhat because of the nature of the writing. The verbal use of the first and second person dramatically arises out of the very fact of these being plays. Of course philosophic writings tend to be, rather, in the third person, might one not argue. To this point I have on reflection decided that an answer is twofold. First, Hume as we have remarked and others do in fact use the first person plural a fair deal; for, in effect, "us human beings". (This is surely a healthy practice. We shall return to considering it below.) Secondly, may the situation of interpersonal life that Shakespeare portrays not be *ipso facto* closer to, not further from, truth, and especially the truth of human living, than any objectivized armchair consideration of it?

53. The passage in full reads:

Malcolm.	Let us seek out some desolate shade, and there
	Weep our sad bosoms empty.
MacDuff.	Let us rather
	Hold fast the mortal sword, and like good men
	Bestride our down-fall'n birthdom. Each new morn,
	New widows howl, new orphans cry; new sorrows
	Strike heaven on the face, that it resounds
	As if it felt with Scotland, and yell'd out
	Like syllable of dolour.
Malcolm.	What I believe, I'll wail;
	What know, believe; and what I can redress,
	As I shall find the time to friend, I will.

I take the beginning of Malcolm's second speech to mean: What I take to heart, I will mourn; and what I am personally acquainted with, I will take to heart. But I shall not bemoan, or revenge, all and sundry indiscriminately. That is: he is not doubting MacDuff's report of the facts; his comment is about how he personally will respond to them. I have used the edition of Henry Cuningham, London: Methuen [1912], 1928, p. 110.

54. *Faith & Belief,* chap. 6, re *All's Well That Ends Well,* 2:3:159: "Believe not thy disdain".

55. Hobbes, *Leviathan,* III. xliii (p. 615).

56. In the concluding sentence (p. 616) of the paragraph from whose opening sentence our cited statement (previous ref.) is taken. Admittedly, this is suggestive rather than conclusive, inasmuch as the word "know" is quoted here, rather than being original with Hobbes. Yet a reading of the paragraph as a whole leaves, I think, no doubt but that the interpretation here proffered is valid.

57. Throughout this discussion, faith and obedience are correlated. The latter is specified as the will to obey (*Leviathan,* p. 611). Cf. also the sequel (pp. 623-24), where in summary both faith and obedience are said to "concurre" in being necessary to salvation, the will to good rendering a man "capable of *living by his Faith*". In one paragraph Hobbes says that God "alwaies" accepts the will to good for good itself, "as well in good, as in evill men"; in the next paragraph, he only seems to contradict this, by saying that God accepts this "onely in the Faithfull". The case of a person who believes (in our sense) without willing to obey is not considered in these pages.

58. The paragraphs that immediately follow lend themselves to propositionalist reading, and could have been so read already in the seventeenth century. That "faith", however, still means also faithfulness, in addition to recognition, and that "beleef" still means faith, at least in significant part, comes out in the discussion a little further along, where "to beleeve, that Jesus is the King" is Hobbes's exegesis of the bidding of "our Saviour", "*come and follow me:* which was as much as to say, Relye on me that am the King" (*Leviathan,* p. 622).

59. That the giving of allegiance is involved, is latent throughout the chapter but emerges more manifestly in that this discussion leads up to a consideration of the problem of the relation between this belief in Jesus as Christ and one's allegiance to the "Civill Soveraign" (*Leviathan,* p. 624). And indeed the entire chapter is introduced with the rubric, "The difficulty of obeying God and Man both at once" (marginal heading to opening paragraph; p. 609). That is, the topic under discussion is loyalty to Jesus, as Christ (where "loyalty" is our twentieth-century word; "beleefe" was his seventeenth-century counterpart) and the obedience due to one's earthly "lawfull Soveraign" (p. 609). Cf. below, our chap. III here, ref. 35.

60. We have conceded that the propositionalist dimension is strong in the discussion of the credal article in question (*Leviathan,* esp. pp. 612-22), with the moral dimension additional to it. In general, on the relation between the two aspects here and in his writing elsewhere, one might make this historical comment, noting that the equivalence here of "beleef" with following, relying on, and with faith, comes in a discussion where the words "faith", "beleef", and "beleeve" occur interchangeably. Taking his work as a whole, one may see Hobbes as operating with notions of "believing" that retain something—in fact, a good deal—from an earlier era when the word denoted trust, self-commitment, and loyalty to a person, and specifically God, but are at the same time increasingly informed by developments of the newer era, in which certainly he was participating, in which the object was beginning to be, rather, more strictly propositional. It is my impression, then, although I have not checked this very far, that the word "faith" comes to his mind more readily as more or less interchangeable with the word "belief" or even is unconsciously preferred to it, but without contradistinction, the more strongly these earlier meanings impinge. Another way of putting this would be to say that in this literature one can observe "belief" beginning its move away from an equivalence with "faith". Cf. further above, at our reff. 12-18, 20-25.

61. *Summa Theologiae,* IIa IIae, quaest. 1, art. 3: *fidei non potest subesse aliquod falsum.* Cf. ibid., ad 2: *prout cadit sub fide, non potest esse falsum.* My copy is the 2nd Lethielleux edition (". . . Theologica"), Paris, 5 voll., n.d. (sc. 1886 ff.), where this is vol. III, page 8.

62. Bacon, *Advancement,* II. xxv. 19 (Case edn., p. 231; Spedding edn., III. 488).

63. Ibid.

64. "Belief and truth of opinion" he has called "the internal soul of religion", with "service and adoration" being "the external body thereof. And therefore the heathen religion was not only a worship of idols, but the whole religion was an idol in itself; for it had no soul, that is, no certainty of belief or confession". That is, doctrines that are not true are for him merely outward forms: what some to-day would call a religion's false beliefs belonged, for him, to a different category altogether from belief. This position has its parallel in various modern conservative Christian thinkers who will not use the word "faith" for religious communities other than the Christian.

65. He notes two kinds of proposition that, he says, we think probable without actually

knowing that they are true: namely, those that "we admit for truth by error of reasoning" and those that we admit "from trusting to other men". Of these, he may call both "opinion" (cf. ref. 22 above) but only the latter "belief"; and he goes on: "Belief, which is the admitting of propositions upon trust, in many cases is no less free from doubt, ..." as cited in our text; and he proceeds to illustrate this by remarking that "there be many things which we receive from report of others, of which it is impossible to imagine any cause of doubt". Hobbes, *Human Nature*, vi. 6, 9; Molesworth edn. (our ref. 22 above), IV. 29-30. (I have omitted italics.) It will be recalled that elsewhere, of the two kinds of proposition mentioned here only the former is called "opinion" (ref. 21 above). In other words, we are witnessing here the first beginnings, not yet firm, of the development where belief was becoming of the same genus with opinion.

66. Locke, *Essay*, IV. xviii. 7, 9 (Fraser, II. 423, 424. Cf. P.-P., p. 357; § 9 is omitted from this latter edition). Cf. IV. xvii. 23 (Fraser, II. 412-13; P.-P., p. 354). (The original has italics.)

67. Ibid., IV. xvi. 14 (Fraser, II. 384; P.-P., p. 343.)(The original has italics.)

68. Ibid., IV. xvi. 14 (Fraser, II. 383; P.-P., p. 343). Similarly, "faith ... leaves no manner of room for doubt or hesitation" (same ref.).

69. Ibid., IV, xv (the title and the topic of the chapter; and the word recurs throughout. Fraser, II. 363-68; P.-P., pp. 334-36). In § iii, he writes "Probability is likeliness to be true" (p. 365/335).

70. In the chapter just mentioned, although in § 1 he writes "a man perceives ..." (Fraser, II. 363; P.-P., p. 334), nonetheless most of the discussion throughout involves the first person, either plural or singular (§ 3 "... arguments or proofs that are found to persuade *us*.... That which makes *me* believe ... the thing *I* believe ..." (p. 365/ 335). Cf. his next chapter: some examples from the concluding paragraph are, "*our* assent ... *our* minds ... *we* must ... *our* assent" (IV. xvi. 14. Fraser II. 383; P.-P., p. 343). Italics here are mine.

71. The title of IV. xx (Fraser, II. 442-59; P.-P., pp. 363-69) is: "Of Wrong Assent, or Error" and these words recur. The word "opinion" is standard throughout this chapter, and is regularly disdainful—especially "common received opinions", which keep many people "in ignorance or error" (§ 17; Fraser, II. 457, 456). Similarly, "erroneous opinions" occurs in the last sentence of the chapter (§ 18; Fraser, II. 459); "opinions ... equally absurd", "any improbable opinion", "an opinion so absurd", "wrong opinions" are also found (§ § 10, 10, 17, 18; Fraser, II. 450, 451, 457, 458). The word "belief", on the other hand, hardly occurs in this discussion of what to-day would be called "wrong beliefs". In fact, it is found once, and then not disdainfully: the context is a trifle ambiguous, but can most easily be read as suggesting a valid belief, an explanation being required for the error of its *not* being adopted. (That explanation is the commonalty's lack of "convenience or opportunity to make experiments and observations themselves, tending to the proof of [the] proposition" [§ 2; Fraser, II. 443]). Indeed, the contrary phrase "ignorance, error, or infidelity [*sic*]" seems to arise naturally (§ 16; Fraser, II. 455).

Something similar to this tendency to use the word "belief" only positively may be observed even in the twentieth century still with the word "faith": this being still, with several, the name of a virtue, many writers might speak of faith, or trust, being misplaced —one can have faith in someone, or even something, unworthy of it—yet they would hardly write spontaneously of faith as in itself wrong. Faith is thought of as a good thing, even though open to abuse; but belief is no longer so to-day.

72. It is always difficult to be sure, and impossible to document, that a given usage

does *not* occur in a large body of writing. I can only report that I have not noted it. Illustratively, as we have just remarked, the word "belief" hardly occurs in the chapter entitled "Of Wrong Assent, or Error" (cf. ref. 71 just above), and not at all as explicitly wrong belief. The verb, which in general seems to have preceded the noun in the gradual loosening of a link with truth, *is* used in this chapter; also not explicitly of believing falsely, yet at times implicitly so.

73. Cf. his discussions on these matters mentioned in ref. 41 above. He speaks of the object of belief as being a matter of fact: "the belief of any matter of fact". Hume, *Treatise*, Appendix; Selby-Bigge edn., p. 628—in some modern editions this addendum is, rather, duly inserted in its proper place as part of I. III. vii: e.g., in the Everyman's Library edition with introduction by A. D. Lindsay, London: Dent, and New York: Dutton, 2 voll. [1911], 1968, where this is I. 99. Again: "Every particular fact is there the object of belief" (Selby-Bigge, p. 625; Lindsay, II. 315). In the latter instance there is involved also the first person singular, displayed in five of the preceding six sentences: "I hear . . . I am acquainted . . . my senses . . . my mind . . . when I recollect . . ." etc. Similarly with the verb: "to believe [*sic*] any matter of fact [*sic*] present to us [*sic*]" (*Treatise*, Appendix; Selby-Bigge, p. [623]; Lindsay, II. 313). Throughout these discussions, the object of both verb and noun tends to be simple, not complex (*pace* Mill). Another instance where his use of "belief", "believe" is–no doubt insouciantly–of a belief that is in fact valid, even though in this case it is not credited, is the funny story (above, ref. 28) about the King of Siam who through lack of personal evidence distrusts the tale about ice, does not "believe" it, although in fact it is true. Belief here once again is the personal acceptance for oneself of a truth.

74. For this Stoic concept, see *Stoicorum Veterum Fragmenta,* collegit Ioannes Ab Arnim, Stutgardiae: Teubner, 4 voll. [1924], 1968, and s.vv. συγκαταθεσις συγκατα-τιθεμαι [*synkatathesis, synkatatithemai*] in *index verborum* . . . , IV. 135-36. For a recent bibliography, see C. J. de Vogel, ed., *Greek Philosophy: A Collection of Texts with Notes and Explanations*, 2nd edn., Leiden: E. J. Brill, 1964, III. 114-16 (§ § 983-84).

75. Hume,*Treatise*, II. III, x; Selby-Bigge edn., p. 453. The continuity of this usage of the first person plural into fairly recent times in William James's discussions of belief, will be discussed in my *Faith & Belief*, chap. 6.

76. *Random House Dictionary* (ref. 35 above), s.v. "belief".

77. [Samuel Langhorne Clemens], *Mark Twain's Notebook, Prepared for Publication with Comments* by Albert Bigelow Paine, New York and London: Harper, 1935, p. 237. The full entry reads: "There are those who scoff at the schoolboy, calling him frivolous and shallow. Yet it was a schoolboy who said: 'Faith is believing what you know ain't so.' "

78. Above, ref. 20.

79. "We talked of belief in ghosts" was cited in the Oxford English Dictionary, s.v. "Belief", 1888, as the first instance of this meaning for the phrase "belief in", from Boswell's *Life* of Johnson, "1790" (sc. 1791). (In George Birkbeck Hill, ed., *Boswell's Life of Johnson*, rev. edn. by L. F. Powell, Oxford: Clarendon [1934], 1964-71, this is I. 405.) Since then, however, the Journal on which this part of the *Life* was based has been found and published, so that the date can now be set back to 1763. See Frederick A. Pottle, ed., *Boswell's London Journal 1762-1763,* London: Heineman, 1951, p. 350 (in the New York, 1950 edition this is p. 284). Cf. Hill, *Boswell,* I. 343 for a similar use of the verb.

80. *Random House Dictionary*, s.v. "belief", in a supplementary section on synonyms.

Chapter III

1. Throughout this chapter, statistics for the King James Authorized version are based on Young, *Concordance* (above, our chap. II, ref. 9). Similarly, I have used John W. Ellison, ed., *Nelson's Complete Concordance of the Revised Standard Version Bible*, New York, Edinburgh, etc.: Nelson, 1957. For the Old Testament Hebrew I have used Solomon Mandelkern, *Veteris Testamenti Concordantiae Hebraicae atque Chaldaicae*, rev. ed., Leipzig: Margolin, 1925; and for the New Testament Greek, Alfred[i] Schmoller, *Concordantiae Novi Testamenti graeci/ Handkonkordanz zum griechischen Neuen Testament*, 14th edn., Stuttgart: Württembergische Bibelanstalt, 1968. For the Biblical texts I have used Rud. Kittel, P. Kahle, edd. (3rd edn., A. Alt, O. Eissfeldt,edd.), *Biblia Hebraica*, Stuttgartiae: Priv. Württ. Bibelanstalt, 1937, and Kurt Aland, Matthew Black, et al., edd., *The Greek New Testament*, 2nd edn., Stuttgart, Amsterdam, London, Edinburgh, New York: United Bible Societies, 1968.

2. Not only English. The concept of faith having been developed as a basic new religious category by the Christian movement, the translating of it into many languages has, of course, posed problems. Speaking of a number of remote languages, whose very names are unfamiliar to most people, two recent authors in a manual on translating the New Testament write, commenting on the rendering of *pisteuō*: "[I]t is not strange that so many terms denoting faith should be highly figurative and represent an almost unlimited range of emotional 'centers' and descriptions of relationships, e.g. 'steadfast his heart' (Chol), 'to arrive on the inside' (Trique), 'to conform with the heart' (Timorese), 'to join the word to the body' (Uduk), 'to hear in the insides' (Kabba-Laka), 'to make the mind big for something' (Putu), 'to make the heart straight about' (Mitla Zapotec), 'to cause a word to enter the insides' (Lacandon), 'to leave one's heart with' (Kuripako), 'to catch in the mind' (Valiente), 'that which one leans on' (Vai), . . ." and so on. Robert G. Bratcher and Eugene A. Nida, *A Translator's Handbook on the Gospel of Mark*, Leiden: E. J. Brill, 1961 (Helps for translators, prepared under the auspices of the United Bible Societies, vol. II), p. 38.

3. Eighteen times the English verb "believe" was used not to render a verb in the Greek but in an English verbal phrase to translate the Greek adjectives πιστος, ἀπιστος [*pistos, apistos*] (9 and 7 times, respectively) and the noun πιστις [*pistis*](twice):"that believe not", and the like. Over against a view that this might seem to weaken our case a little, one could equally see it as strengthening it, it being the more evident then that for these translators the verb "believe" was the equivalent of "to be faithful", "to have faith", or however we might word a verbal mode with "faith".

It should be noted further that there is one instance where "faith" in the 1611 English renders not the root πιστ- [*pist-*] but rather the noun ἐλπις [*elpis*], normally "hope": namely, Hebrews 10:23. Similarly, "believe" (also, "unbelief") renders not *pist-* but the cognate πειθεω, ἀπειθεω, ἀπειθεια [*peitheō, apeitheō, apeitheia*]15 times. In the Old Testament, one of the "faith"-family words in the English—namely, "faithfulness"—out of 56 times renders once not the root *āman, heʾemîn* but rather כון [*k-w-n*] "to be firm" (Psalm 5:9, in the English; 5:10 in the Hebrew).

4. *The New English Bible: New Testament*, London: Oxford University Press/ Cambridge University Press, 1961. I have used the "Popular Edition".

5. Henri Monnier, *La Mission historique de Jésus*, 2ᵉ édn., Paris: Fischbacher, 1914, p. 176.

6. William Henry Paine Hatch, *The Pauline Idea of Faith, in its Relation to Jewish and Hellenistic Religion*, Cambridge: Harvard University Press, and London: Oxford

University Press (George F. Moore et al., edd., Harvard Theological Studies, II), 1917, pp. 23, 24n.

7. Joseph A. Fitzmyer, in *The Jerome Biblical Commentary*, Raymond E. Brown, Joseph A. Fitzmyer, Roland E. Murphy, edd., Englewood Cliffs, N.J.: Prentice-Hall, 1968, one-vol. edn., p. 821.

8. "For Paul the primary meaning of faith (πιστις [*pistis*]) is obedience (ὑπακοη [*hypakoē*])". Rudolph Bultmann, *Das Urchristentum im Rahmen der antiken Religionen*, Zurich: Artemis, 1949 (Walter Rüegg, ed., Erasmus-Bibliothek), p. 256 (*Primitive Christianity in Its Contemporary Setting*, R. H. Fuller, trans., London and New York: Thames and Hudson, 1956, p. 231), note 26.

9. In the ὁτι [*hoti*] clause there are quite a number of variant readings:

εἰς ἐστιν ὁ θεος

εἰς ὁ θεος ἐστιν

ὁ θεος εἰς ἐστιν

etc.; the use of the definite article pushes the meaning further in the direction of our argument, but we let that pass. It is the πιστευεις and πιστευουσιν [*pisteueis* and *pisteuousin*] that are here in question.

10. Matthew 26:70, 72; Mark 14:68, 70—Luke 22:57—John 13:38; and John 18:25, 27.

11. Acts 3:13, 14.

12. The root here is *k-f-r*, which means to repudiate, to spurn, to reject, and is indeed remarkably counterpart to Biblical ἀρνεομαι [*arneomai*]. The usage of the Arabic term and its conceptual presupposing of the validity of what is rejected are discussed at length in my *Faith & Belief*, chap. 3. On this term see also Marilyn Robinson Waldman, "The Development of the Concept of *kufr* in the Qur'an", *Journal of the American Oriental Society*, 88:442-55 (1968).

13. *Philippi Melanthonis Opera quae Supersunt Omnia*, ed. Carolus Gottlieb Bretschneider, Halis Saxonum: Schwetschke, vol. xiii [1846] (Bretschneider, ed., Corpus Reformatorum, 1834-60, vol. xiii), coll. 216-18. I have used the 1963 reprint, New York and London: Johnson, and Frankfurt am Main: Minerva. It is illegitimate to dismiss Melanchthon as obtuse or obscurantist: he was a leading humanist, and did much in general to spread the new learning. Apart from his important role in the setting up of the German public school system, it is interesting to note his vigorous appeal for a study of the natural world, despite our inability to arrive at any but partial knowledge about it, as morally and divinely incumbent upon man. This appears, for instance, in his dedicatory epistle prefixed to the very work, *Initia doctrinae physicae*, 1549, from which the above is taken: a letter to Michael Meienburg. See Bretschneider, vol. vii [1840], coll. 472-73. He does not actually choose the Latin word *imaginor*, but uses *confingo*, "to fabricate, feign, invent" (*hi ludi conficti sunt*—xiii. 216).

It is instructive to note how the situation had begun to change by the following century. Bacon felt quite firmly that the Copernican theory was wrong (*falsissimum*—*De Augm.*, III. 4; see "a" below); nonetheless he recognized that many in his society had meanwhile come to accept it. (That way of thinking, he acknowledges, "has gained strength" [*invaluit*: ibid., IV. 1—"b" below].) That is, he himself holds it to be wrong, but can no longer take for granted that it is wrong, or that his readers will do so. Accordingly, in speaking of it he normally uses in English the word "opinion", and in Latin, *opinio* and *sententia*: ". . . the opinion of Copernicus in astronomy, which . . . natural philosophy doth correct" (*Val. Term.*, I. 8—"c")—or, in another place, amending

this, "... may correct" (*Advancement*, II. ix. 1—"d"); and in the revised Latin version
several years later: *constat sententiam Copernici de Rotatione Terrae ... revinci ...
posse* (*De Augm.*, IV. 1—"e"). He speaks elsewhere also of the *opinio de motu terrae* and
of the *opinio ... de sole ut sit centrum mundi et immobile ... a Copernico introducta*
(*Globi*, vi—"f"). He calls the position, also, a *concessum non concessibile* (*Nov. Org.*II. 46—
"g": "a giving in to what cannot be given in to"). He asks whether the motion
attributed by Copernicus and his followers to the earth be not something found in
nature but rather (using also Melanchthon's word) something fictitious and imaginary
(*an potius res conficta sit et supposita: Nov. Org.*, II. 36—"h"). Again, he refers to the
idea as thought up rather irresponsibly (*rotationem terrae, quod etiam satis licenter
excogitatum est—De Fluxu:* "j"). He uses the verb *placet* also: *eos quibus terram rotari
placet* (*Globi*, v—"k"); ... *quod Copernico placuit* (ibid., vi—"l").
The references for the above are more fully as follows, with in each case page
references in parentheses to the Spedding edition (above, our chap. II, ref. 11):
(a) *De Dignitate et Augmentis Scientiarum* [London: Joannes Haviland, 1623] (I.552)
(b) *De Dignitate* ... (I. 580)
(c) *Valerius Terminus, of the Interpretation of Nature: With the Annotations of
Hermes Stella,* [first published about a century after Bacon's death by Robert
Stephens, London, 1734] (III. 229)
(d) *Of the Proficience and Advancement of Learning Divine and Humane,* [London:
Henrie Tomes, 1605] (III. 367; in the Case edn., p. 114)
(e) *De Dignitate* ... (I. 580)
(f) *Descriptio Globi Intellectualis* (written about 1612? —see Ellis, in Spedding, III.
715; published posthumously) [London, ed. Gruter, 1653] (III. 741)
(g) *Novum Organum* (sc. Part II of the *Instauratio Magna*) [London: *apud* Joannem
Billium, 1620] (I. 327)
(h) *Novum Organum* (I. 297)
(j) *De Fluxu et Refluxu Maris* ("probably written before or not long after 1616"—
Ellis, in Spedding, III.44) [London, ed. Gruter, 1653] (III.53)
(k) *Descriptio Globi Intellectualis* (cf. "f" above) (III. 734)
(l) *Descriptio* ... (III. 742)
I have found helpful, but by no means adequate, the Spedding index (V. 579, s.v.
Copernicus; cf. V. 585, s.v. Earth, rotation of the); to its entries at least the following
should be added: I. 297, 327, 552, 580; III. 367, 741, 742; IV. 183; V. 515, 518.
[Later: Add also entries s.vv. Terra, Rotatio, Rotation.]
14. Strictly, this is too hasty. His view approximated to truth more closely than the
Ptolemaic that it replaced; nonetheless it was still a distant approximation. If he
believed ("imagined") that the sun was the centre of the universe (and even this is an
over-simplification: in order to square with his calculations, he placed the sun at a little
distance from his postulated centre), he was, we now "know", wrong. Some call his
theory "heliostatic" rather than "heliocentric", to take account of that eccentricity. Yet
we now know the sun to be even more vagrant than he envisaged the earth as being.
15. Nicolai Copernici *de Hypothesibus Motuum Coelestium a se Constitutis Commen-
tariolus,* c. 1510? [first published in printed form, 1878].   The Preface printed with
the *De Revolutionibus* [1543], presenting the thesis as explicitly an hypothesis, was
written, it is now agreed, not by Copernicus but anonymously by his friend and champion
the Lutheran theologian Andreas Osiander. (The word *hypothesis* does occur occasionally in Copernicus's own 1543 text; e.g., in the chapter-title of III. iii, and that
chapter's opening paragraph.)

16. It is not, I suppose, logically impossible (though we may cheerfully doubt that it has ever happened) that one might imagine a non-existent class of devils who in turn are thought of as imagining a class of divine beings that explicitly does not exist, not only not in the real world as conceived by the person performing this feat but also not in the imaginary world postulated by him as inhabited by his devils. These last could even be thought of as trembling because of their imputed dream-world. I do suggest, however, that it would be if not a logical contradiction, at least a markedly weak argument, to use such a conjecture in a contention such as the one that James is here putting forward. It is virtually impossible, historically, to imagine such a fantasy as happening in the first century A.D., yet I suppose that theoretically one could picture an argument that would run something like this: "There are no gods; but it is useful for the masses to believe in them nonetheless, to keep themselves moral. We may imagine a class of devils who believe in such non-existent gods and who are nonetheless not moral; but do not you be like them". The response might come back, "Why not?"—and it is in an answer to this last question that faith might find itself involved.

17. "For the good that I would I do not: but the evil which I would not, that I do" (Romans 7:19; cf. 7:15, and that chapter in general). Indeed, St. Paul had been plagued by a feeling of man's incapacity before the moral law (*tôrāh, nomos*): the sense of a yawning gap between perception and performance seems to have haunted him, and through him St. Augustine, and the Puritans. On the other hand, as a Christian, St. Paul gained a quite new and joyous sense of that gap's closure: the good news was for him, in significant part, the bridging of it in faith. (I have been helped to see something of this latter aspect of St. Paul, otherwise obscured for me by the vehemence of his other position, by C. H. Dodd, *The Epistle of Paul to the Romans* [London: Hodder & Stoughton, 1932] London: Collins, Fontana, 1965, commentary on 6:1-8:13, "The New Life in Christ", pp. 104-43.) The man of faith of St. Paul, and the man of insight of Socrates, perhaps converge more than we have recognized.

18. In discussing this passage here and in the next paragraph, I have in general presented the English translation of the Revised Standard Version, in double quotation marks. Where I feel that the New English Bible more clearly interprets the meaning, I use its wording, in single quotation marks. (An exception to this last is that I have myself introduced the capitalization of the *T* in "Truth" for verse 12.) Rendering the noun and verb πιστ- [*pist-*], I give my own translation in italics.

19. John Locke, in "A Letter to Anthony Collins, Esq." dated October 29, 1703. *The Works of John Locke: A New Edition, Corrected, in Ten Volumes* [London: Tegg *et al.*, also Glasgow: Griffin, and Dublin: Cumming, 1823], X, 271. I have used the Aalen: Scientia Verlag, 1963 reprint.

20. Ayer, *Central Questions* (above, our chap. I, ref. 7), concluding sentence (p. 235). One may note, however, that in his Preface, Sir Alfred acquiesces in the language of the Gifford Trust to the point of allowing himself to be dubbed an earnest inquirer after truth (p. [ix]) (—in unconscious contradistinction from those whom Nielsen sees as less disinterested: cf. above, our chap. I, ref. 3).

21. IV. xix. 1 (Fraser edn. [above, our chap. II, ref. 26], II. 428-29; P.-P., p. 359, omitting the comma before "for"). This chapter, "Of Enthusiasm", appeared first in the 1700 edition of the *Essay*.

22. Locke, "Letter to Collins," 1823 edn., X. 271.

23. Lady Damaris Masham, to whose country home in Essex Locke retired not long after his return to England following his political exile in Holland; in a letter written (January 12, "1704-5", sc., 1705 New Style) two or three months after his death to

their mutual friend Jean Le Clerc, major Biblical scholar and encyclopaedist. The contents of the letter were published by Le Clerc (without acknowledgement) in his "Eloge de feu Mr. Locke" in his *Bibliothèque Choisie* (Amsterdam, 28 voll., 1703-13), 6:342-411 (1705), and an English version of this French version was published as a pamphlet in London the following year: *The Life and Character of Mr. John Locke, Author of the Essay concerning Humane Understanding, Written in French, by Mr. Le Clerc, and Done into English by T. F. P.*, London: for John Clark, at the Bible and Crown, 1706. [A second edition appeared in 1713, but I have not seen it.] Most of the letter was published more or less in its original form from the manuscript in the library of the Remonstrants' College, Amsterdam (where Le Clerc was librarian) in H. R. Fox Bourne, *The Life of John Locke*, London: Henry S. King, 2 voll., 1876, where this sentence appears opposite the title-pages of both volumes and at II, 540 (with slight variations of spelling and punctuation).

24. The concept of person comes into Western civilization from Chrstian theology, which in turn developed it in part from Greek metaphysics. Those whose thinking prefers to move in the opposite direction from that given in our text might wish to say that in Western civilization the concept 'God' has been an hypostatization (the word is not a pun) of the ideal qualities perceived in human personality. The notion of 'ideal' being metaphysical, however, it is not clear that this way of putting the same point is an improvement. There are interesting questions (to which Feuerbach was not alert) not only as to how one (or one's society) is able to perceive such qualities, but also as to whether one is right or wrong in perceiving them, and in regarding them as ideal. In any case, the historical situation is that the Western habit of thinking of human beings explicitly as 'persons', as a term of dignity, was popularized largely from the Christian affirmation that God is a Trinity of three Persons (Greek, προσωπον [*prosōpon*], ὑποστασις [*hypostasis*]; Latin, *persona*), and in particular from the discussions revolving around the teaching (formalized by the Council of Chalcedon, A.D. 451) that Jesus Christ is one 'person' with two natures (human and divine). The fundamental definition of 'person' that prevailed all through the Middle Ages was that propounded by Boethius (ca. 480-524; "the last of the Roman philosophers, and the first of the scholastic theologians") in the course of a Christological disquisition making nice discriminations among the metaphysical notions 'essence', 'existence', 'substance', 'subsistence', 'nature', and 'person'. His wording was: *naturae rationabilis indiuidua substantia*—"a substance that is individual of a nature that is rational". Only gradually did the concept move from being this sort of philosophic and theological technical term to a general characterization for ordinary human beings of themselves and of others. Many Westerners are unaware how characteristic of Western culture is the concept of person. Not only its rise and its development in the latter part of the first millennium A.D., but also the emergence, towards the very end of the second, of a radically different concept of the person (the word is retained, and still bears some of its former freight) in present-day reductionist world-views of a scientist sort, are matters of momentous historical significance. Fortunately, of this last the concomitant depersonalizing [*sic*] tendencies of modern society are not going unnoticed, and one may hope that the trends have not gone so far as to have become irreversible. That the tendencies are correlated with the decline in theology and metaphysics seems to some historically and philosophically obvious; by others it is at least worth reflection.

Apart from Boethius, a major contribution to the early development was made earlier that same century by St. Augustine, who in turn drew some of his conceptualizations and orientations from Plotinus (A.D. 204 or 205 to 270) as well as from Plato and Aristotle;

chiefly in his *De Trinitate*, which continued to be read for centuries, its salient term *persona* being understood in slightly new ways as those centuries proceeded (as, indeed, one might allow oneself to speculate that his term *trinitas* also perhaps was, gradually, coming to be understood as "the Trinity", whereas earlier it was read perhaps as "a trinity" ["God is a trinity"] and when he wrote it the book's title perhaps signified even "on threeness", "on triadicity"?—after all, it is concerned with a triadic quality of the human soul, as well as of God).

Christian writers who in the first half of this present century drew attention to the role of Christian theology in the rise of the Western concept 'person' tended unfortunately to do so by contrasting it with classical thinking, which has led in turn more recently to a classicist tendency to rebut—on both sides as if the two were alternatives, whereas Christian theology in general and Boethius in conspicuous particular represent a confluence, the more notable to-day when the metaphysical and the Christian traditions in the West are both being eroded. De Vogel cites Panaetius (second century B.C.) as a Greek employing our term in a powerful and moving passage, lost in Greek so that one does not know what his actual wording was, but Cicero (first century B.C.) quotes him and uses the Latin *persona* ("role"? "nature"?) to do so. (Each of us, he says, is endued by nature with, as it were, two *personae*, one generically human and one individual: *duabus quasi nos a natura indutos esse personis; quarum una communis est . . . altera . . . proprie singulis est tributa.* This is not yet our concept of person, but is on its way towards it [although some might translate: "each of us is allotted two roles to play", or even: ". . . has two masks put on him . . ."].) Along with the recently growing recognition of the power, profundity, and significance of the thought of Plotinus has gone also an awareness of this "pagan" thinker's historical influence, not least on Augustine. The forging of the Western concept of person in the Middle Ages was done by Christian thinkers not single-handed, but drawing as ever on the rich heritage of Greek metaphysics and metaphysical humanism as well as on the Biblical, and on their own creativity.

For Panaetius see Cicero, *De Officiis,* scattered passages brought together in C. J. de Vogel, *Greek Philosophy: A Collection of Texts with Notes and Explanations,* vol. III: *The Hellenistic-Roman Period,* 2nd edn., Leiden: Brill, 1964, p. 243. On this matter in Plotinus, see *inter multa alia* A. H. Armstrong, "Form, Individual and Person in Plotinus", forthcoming with Bibliography. For St. Augustine—apart from his own *De Trinitate* (e.g.: *Sancti Aurelii Augustini de Trinitate libri xv*, W. J. Mountain, Fr. Glorie, edd., Turnholti: Brepols, 2 voll., 1968 [Corpus Christianorum series Latina, 50, 50a: Aurelii Augustini Opera, 16])—see Charles Norris Cochrane, *Christianity and Classical Culture: A Study of Thought and Action from Augustus to Augustine,* London: Oxford University Press [1940; rev. edn., 1944]; especially chapter xi, "Nostra Philosophia: the Discovery of Personality" (the word "discovery" is unfortunate). I have used the paperback edn.: New York: Oxford, Galaxy, 1966, where this is pp. 399-455. See also, more recently (but perhaps less plausibly), Paul Henry, *Saint Augustine on Personality,* New York: Macmillan, 1960 (Robert P. Russell, ed., The Saint Augustine Lecture Series, Villanova University, 1959).

On Boethius: Anicii Manlii Severini Boethii, . . . *liber Contra Eutychen et Nestorium . . . Iohanni Diacono.* The definition is found in chap. 3, opening sentence. (I have used the 1926 reprint of the Loeb Classical Library edition: H. F. Stewart and E. K. Rand, edd. and transs., *Boethius: The Theological Tractates* . . . London: Heinemann, and New York: Putnam, 1918. The definition is pp. 84-85; the English version given above is, however, my own. The above characterization of the author is from the Introduction, p. x.)

More generally, and for the later period, see Étienne Gilson, *The Spirit of Mediaeval*

Philosophy (Gifford Lectures 1931-32), A. H. C. Downes, trans., London: Sheed & Ward, and New York: Scribner's [1936], 1940, chap. X, "Christian Personalism", pp. 189-208, 464-67. These lectures (delivered in English?) were written in French and translated by another hand, evidently; the French version: Étienne Gilson, *L'Esprit de la philosophie médiévale*, Paris: Vrin, 1932.

For an exposition of the classicist side of what has developed into a debate, see de Vogel, *Greek Philosophy*, III. xii-xiii; and for the implementing of her final sentence in that passage ("I hope to expound this question more explicitly"), see C. J. de Vogel, "The Concept of Personality in Greek and Christian Thought", in John K. Ryan, ed., *Studies in Philosophy and the History of Philosophy*, Washington, D.C.: Catholic University of America Press, 2:20-60 (1963). She, however, does not distinguish, as do I, between concept and conception, explicit and implicit; even perhaps, to some degree, form and content. It seems quite obvious that Western civilization's understanding of human beings, including in the mediaeval period but more markedly so of course in the early modern, has been greatly coloured by the heritage of Greek humanism, not least as set forth in, for instance, Greek drama.

Gilson, against whom in particular Miss de Vogel reacts, despite his disclaimer (pp. 206-8), perhaps overstates his case (and presents also a perhaps overly individualistic conception of the person). Yet he has something of a point, in that the assertion of St. Thomas Aquinas with which his analysis culminates, *persona significat id quod est perfectissimum in tota natura*, " 'person' signifies that which is most perfect in the whole of nature", could readily be translated into any of the languages of modern Christendom but not so readily into classical Greek nor into those of most others of the world's cultures, and counterparts to it would prove illuminatingly divergent from each other and from it. (The Sanskrit term *puruṣa* would teasingly give pause.) Nonetheless, Gilson definitely under-appreciated (more bluntly: ignored) Plotinus. This is eloquently, if tacitly, shown in, for instance, this comment on what he calls Christian personalism: "Thus we are carried far beyond Greek thought, whether it be Plato's or Aristotle's" (p. 202).

For a modern analyst's hesitations about attributing a full-blown statement of our concept to the *De Trinitate*, see A. C. Lloyd, "On Augustine's Concept of a Person", in R. A. Markus, ed., *Augustine: A Collection of Critical Essays*, Garden City, N.Y.: Doubleday (Amelie Oksenberg Rorty, gen. ed., Modern Studies in Philosophy), 1972, pp. [191]-[205]. This may be seen as in refutation of P. Henry, above; it does not seriously touch the historical thesis here presented that Augustine's writing was seminal for the subsequent elaboration of the concept in European thought.

The Latin quotation by Gilson from Aquinas is from *Summa Theologiae*, I:29:3: response. (Lethielleux edn.[above, our chap. II, ref. 61], vol. I, p. 174.)

25. *hsin.* 信

26. See, for example, the 1909 "Supplement", *Jesus or Christ?*, to the *Hibbert Journal*, London: Williams & Norgate, and Boston: Sherman, French, 1909.

27. David Friedrich Strauss, *Der Christus des Glaubens und der Jesus der Geschichte: eine Kritik des Schleiermacher'schen Lebens Jesu*, Berlin: Franz Duncker, 1865. I have not seen the original, but have consulted the copy in Widener Library, Harvard University, "reproduced by Duopage Process, Cleveland, Ohio: Bell & Howell".

28. Exact counting is difficult, since there are some ambiguities. For instance, in John 6:47 the best text seems to read ὁ πιστευων ἐχει ζωην αἰωνιον [*ho pisteuōn ekhei zōen aiōnion*] ("he that has faith has life transcendent"), but several manuscripts have the variant reading πιστευων εἰς ἐμε [*pisteuōn eis eme*] (". . . faith in [-to] me").Another

kind of ambiguity is John 6:69, where the translators of the New English Bible take πεπιστευκαμεν [*pepisteukamen*] absolutely ("We have faith"—this is followed by a comma, which the next verb is not, in such a way that the former is disjoined from the "that" clause which becomes then the object of only the following "we know": "We have faith, and we know that . . ."). This understanding makes our verb co-ordinate with the two preceding instances of its use in this passage (verse 64). Yet one need not choose this interpretation; and the Revised Standard Version elects the alternative (although its "We have believed, and have come to know, that . . ." is strange in modern English--unless it should be taken to mean: "We used to believe, but now we have come to know, that . . .", which is certainly not in the Greek, and is not intended). I have not counted an instance such as I Corinthians 11:18.

29. Luke 18:8. Matthew 6:30—Luke 12:28; Matthew 8:26, also 16:8; cf. 14:31. Matthew 9:22—Mark 5:34—Luke 8:48; Mark 10:52—Luke 18:42; also Luke 7:50 and 17:19. I Corinthians 13:13. Hebrews 11:8, 11, 23. It is worth noting, in passing, that in the case of the third group of passages here the 1611 translators rendered the same Greek words, occurring seven times in the text (ἡ πιστις σου σεσωκεν σε [*hē pistis sou sesōken se*]), indifferently as "thy faith hath made thee whole" and "thy faith hath saved thee" (five times and twice respectively). This would suggest that in their minds the concepts 'salvation' and even 'faith' signified something relatively remote from what they both implied for most English-speaking persons in the nineteenth century and relatively close to what I in the latter twentieth am proposing here as a reconstruction for what they meant in the first. Cf. Luther at the end of this paragraph in our text.

30. In Catholic thought, it is my impression that throughout the Middle Ages the dominant custom was for the concept *fides* to be used without specification. Of course, even if this be factually correct, the interpretation of it is open to discussion. The issue is a large one indeed. I have elsewhere developed fairly carefully (e.g., my *Faith & Belief*, chap. 5) a thesis that pre-modern Christian writers appear not to have thought explicitly of "Christian faith" because they were unaware of any other kind. They thought of faith absolutely, as something that had become available to mankind only, or virtually only, through Christ and the Church. The recent discovery that it is available through other traditions is something that Church thinking has as yet hardly even the vocabulary to ponder. My Cadbury Lectures at the University of Birmingham in 1972, "Towards a Theology of Comparative Religion", were addressed to this issue; and my *Meaning and End of Religion* (above, chap. II. ref. 2) was a prolegomenon. I have examined in some degree the history of specificationist concepts, such as the use of the phrase "Christian faith", the use of a plural "faiths", and in English the use of an article (for instance, whether to translate Latin *fides* as "faith" or as "the faith"). I have not, however, done any close historical study for the post-Biblical centuries of the concept of an object of faith, except for St. Thomas Aquinas, for whom that object is always God, and of whom more below.

31. Friedrich Schleiermacher, *Der christliche Glaube, nach den Grundsätzen der evangelischen Kirche in Zusammenhange dargestellt* [Berlin: Reimer, 1821, 1830²], 7te Auflage, Martin Redeker, herausgeb., 2 Bde, Berlin: de Gruyter, 1960. Id., *The Christian Faith*, Eng. Trans. of the 2nd German edn., H. R. Mackintosh, J. S. Stewart, edd., Edinburgh: T. & T. Clark, [1928] 1968. It can be shown that in the early nineteenth century the words of the title denoted "Christian faith" (more fully, "the Christian form of faith"). A hundred years later, it was interpreted rather as "the Christian faith". See a forthcoming article, by the present writer, on the nuances of this particular translation.

32. In the sayings of Jesus the noun πιστις [*pistis*] occurs 21 times. The compounds ὀλιγοπιστος, ὀλιγοπιστια [*oligopistos, - ia*] are found another 6, and ἀπιστος [apistos] 5 times. The adjective πιστος [*pistos*] (usually rendered "faithful") appears a further 9 times (e.g.: "good and faithful servant"). These last, however, many might wish to regard as special, hardly to be counted in the argument (although this begs our question). The singleton phrase "faith in God" (πιστιν θεου [*pistin theou*]) comes in Mark 11:22. (One might speculate about translating it, rather, "faith from God", "divine faith"?)

33. Matthew 8:10—Luke 7:9. Matthew 17:20—Luke 17:6.

34. Oscar Cullmann, *Les Premières confessions de foi chrétiennes,* Paris: Presses Universitaires de France [1943], 1948. "[L]e point de départ et le centre de la foi chrétienne, c'est la foi en Christ" (p. 40); "sa personne est l'objet central de la foi" (p. 41); "Conclusion.... le point de départ historique et le centre dogmatique de la foi chrétienne, c'est la foi en Jésus-Christ" (p. 52). This is "L'essence de la foi chrétienne" (title of chap. iv, p. 39). (For the English [and German] version of this work, and of these passages, see our ref. 44 below.)

35. He makes the telling point that the affirmation "Christ is Lord" owes its reverberating significance, and perhaps its origin, to the contrast with the Roman empire's formula "Caesar is Lord". To the dismay of the uncomprehending Romans, early Christians were willing to die rather than to pronounce the latter simple phrase. For for them, there was one Lord: namely, Christ; and their "confessing" this was for them an act [*sic*] of ultimate import. (Cf. Hobbes above, our chap. II, ref. 59.) I must not be misunderstood as minimizing the significance of the early Christians' faith being in Christ, in this and similar senses. I am asking, however: what is this "faith" that enables, compels, one who has it towards Christ to be loyal to Him even before the lions? Or is "faith" another name of that very loyalty? In his footnote (p. 22, ref. 47) on his passage (*Premières Confessions,* pp. 21-22) setting forth this point, Cullmann remarks: "De même, la foi est définie couramment comme s'adressant au Kyrios", and cites I Corinthians 1:2; Colossians 2:6; Acts 2:36; 9:35; 11:17, 20; 16:31; 20:21. It is the word "définie" here that is at issue, only.

36. He sidesteps, however, the reverberating question—of enormous importance theologically, historically, comparatively, even psychologically—whether the faith of the early Church was faith in God. He does so by remarking, almost as an afterthought, that this is subsumed. (A single sentence, in his two-page *Conclusion*: "Il faut savoir, certes, que le point de départ historique et le centre dogmatique de la foi chrétienne, c'est la foi en Jésus-Christ, mais il faut savoir aussi que cette foi, loin d'exclure la foi en Dieu le Père, lui donne, au contraire, son fondement chrétien, et il en est de même pour le Saint-Esprit" —[Cullmann, *Premières confessions,* p. 52].)

37. In another work, he does deal with it, and makes clear that he takes, in fact, a markedly performative view of faith. He speaks of it as a decision, as an aligning of oneself (with the new historical development that Christ inaugurated). See Oscar Cullmann, *Heil als Geschichte: heilsgeschichtliche Existenz im Neuen Testament,* Tübingen: J. C. B. Mohr (Paul Siebeck) [1965], 1967. (Some examples, from many: ... *die freie Entscheidung, mich in das biblische Geschehen so einzureihen*—p. 306; *Entscheidung für Christus*—p. 305; [*die*] *Entscheidung des Glaubens,* pp. 297-98, 299, and often. In addition to *sich einzureihen,* often, he regularly uses also *sich hineinzustellen*: e.g., pp. 236, 299.) It is true that he speaks at times of the decision, the aligning of oneself, as "flowing from" faith; but at other times, vice versa, he speaks of that decision as evidently a prerequisite to faith. (... *aus diesem Glauben fliesst die Entscheidung,* ...— p. 299; and yet *Um mit ihm im Glauben verbunden zu sein, haben wir* ... *für die Heilsgeschichte zu entscheiden,* p. 301).

38. Hebrews 12:2.

39. Acts 17:6.

40. Thomas Aquinas, *Summa Theologiae*, IIa IIae, quaest. 17, art. 2. (Lethielleux edn., vol. III, pp. 94-95).

41. *Summa Theologiae*, II. II. 57. 1 (Lethielleux, vol. III, pp. 284-85). To the angelic doctor's use of the term "object" with the virtues (and indeed with human actions generally), there is devoted an excursus in one of the more recent volumes in the current Blackfriars' edition of the Latin text with English translation of the larger *Summa*. The treatment is otherwise not fully satisfying, but it does obliquely recognize for our day that the word has for "many minds" (p. 178) changed its usage substantially in the centuries since Aquinas, whose meaning for it is discussed. See T. C. O'Brien, "Objects and Virtues", being Appendix I in Thomas Gilby, gen. ed.: St. Thomas Aquinas, *Summa Theologiae*, Blackfriars—London: Eyre & Spottiswoode, and New York: McGraw Hill, 60 voll., 1964-, vol. 31 (1974), pp. 178-85.

42. St. Paul speaks scores of times of persons being or living "in Christ"; and often of Christ being or "living" or "dwelling" in us—e.g., Romans 8:10; Galatians 2:20 (cf. 4:19); Ephesians 3:17. Cf. St. John, where the English "dwell" translates a different Greek verb from this last ($\mu\epsilon\nu\omega$ rather than $\kappa\alpha\tauο\iota\kappa\epsilon\omega$ [*menō*, "remain", rather than *katoikeō*, "settle down"]): "God dwelleth in us . . . we dwell in Him . . . God dwelleth in him, and he in God"; and, in a perhaps more down-to-earth mysticism, "he that dwelleth in love dwelleth in God"; "the truth . . . dwelleth in us" (I John 4:12-16; II John:2). St. Paul's usage $\pi\iota\sigma\tau ο\iota\varsigma$ $\dot{\epsilon}\nu$ $X\rho\iota\sigma\tau\ omega$ 'Ιησου [*pistois en Christōi Iēsou*] ("faithful in Christ Jesus"), Ephesians 1:1, should also be noted. Similarly (to follow up the preceding paragraph in our text, on faith "in Christ"), in Ephesians 1:13 it is surely almost arbitrary to read $\dot{\epsilon}\nu$ $\dot{\omega}$ . . . $\pi\iota\sigma\tau\epsilon\upsilon\sigma\alpha\nu\tau\epsilon\varsigma$ [*en hōi . . . pisteusantes*] by taking the first two words as an indirect object of the third, rather than as locative, given the seven other locative uses of that same phrase and of $\dot{\epsilon}\nu$ $\tau\omega$ $X\rho\iota\sigma\tau\omega$, $\dot{\epsilon}\nu$ $\alpha\dot{\upsilon}\tau\omega$ [*en tōi Christōi, en autōi*], etc. in this and the immediately preceding verses.

43. The notion of co-subjectivity perhaps has applicability even outside theistic circles of ideas. One might imagine a secular humanist toying with an identifying of faith as what happens (or: has happened?) in a person when he or she sees and feels reality and the universe not as object but as subject, with oneself then as co-subject. The faithlessness of modern life, *vis-à-vis* its ecological, socio-technological, commercial-industrial, environment would be thus illuminated? The ability, in particular, to see and to relate to other persons always and fully not objectively but co-subjectively is, such a view might readily hold, a central part of faith. Cf. also above, our chap. I. ref. 11.

44. Although the phrase "content of faith" has become a trifle current, not only does it seem fairly recent; also, I am not sure whether my impression be correct that its acceptance and spread have been on the whole rather inadvertent, at least in English. The history of its counterparts in other languages I have not grasped; I suspect that there too it is a recent phenomenon, but I should be grateful to be corrected on this if I be wrong. I have found some reason to suppose that it has found its way into English via translations from the Continent. I do not know that any leading theological thinker in English has opted for this, to me markedly problematic, conceptualization.

The most engaging instance of its use in translation is in the case of Cullmann's *Premières confessions* (our ref. 34 above). This thinker's *la foi* (*passim*) comes out in English as "faith" and in German as *der Glaube*, naturally; his *objet . . . de la foi* (once only?—French, p. 41) as the "object of faith" (English, p. 50) and *das . . . Objekt des Glaubens* (German, p. 45); but his *la croyance* and *les croyances* (both, p. 40) emerge in English as "content of faith", "contents of faith" (p. 49) and in German as *Glaubensge-*

halt, Glaubensgehalte (p. 44). Furthermore, [*l'*]*essentiel dans le message* bequeathed by the first generations of Christians (p. 39) is rendered in English as "the essential content [*sic*] of the Gospel" (p. 48) and in German as [*der*] *Wesensinhalt der Botschaft* (p. 43); and even his *l'essence de la foi chrétienne* (title of chap. 4, p. 39) turns up in German as *der Wesensinhalt des christlichen Glaubens* (p. 43). Cullmann himself seems never to affect a phrase *le contenu de la foi,* although the matter is complicated in that I have used the second edition of his French, the first (same publishers, 1943) proving inaccessible to me despite my best efforts, whereas from it (presumably) the versions were taken: Oscar Cullmann, *Die ersten christlichen Glaubensbekenntnisse, aus dem Französischen übersetzt von* V. D. M. *Hans Schaffert,* Zürich: Zollikon, 1943; Oscar Cullmann, *The Earliest Christian Confessions,* J. K. S. Reid, trans., London: Lutterworth, 1949. If it should turn out that the translators were reproducing more faithfully than appears a text from which they were working, then the problem becomes the more engaging, since this would confront us with a movement not towards the "content" notion on the part of the translators but away from it on the part of Cullmann himself.

One finds an explicit statement that *la croyance* is *le contenu de la foi* (at another place: *son contenu intellectuel*), which duly comes out in English as "belief . . . is the content" of faith ("its intellectual content"), in the volume of faith in the bilingual and presumably reasonably authoritative *Encyclopédie du catholique au XXème siècle/ The Twentieth Century Encyclopedia of Catholicism,* in this case the French being original: Eugène Joly, *Qu'est-ce que croire?,* Paris: Arthème Fayard, 1956, p. 127; Eugène Joly, *What Is Faith?,* Illtyd Trethowan, trans., New York: Hawthorn, [1958] 1960, p. 131. This equation makes the "content" of faith different from the "object" of faith, except where the latter has come to be (which it is emphatically not for Joly) propositional. It also offers a solution to the problem of the relation of belief to faith strikingly different from that propounded in my *Faith & Belief,* or adumbrated here.

The most serious and elaborate (yet even it not fully thought-out) instance of this matter, however, that I have encountered is in the work of the leading Swedish Lutheran theologian Gustaf Aulén, who uses the Swedish term *innehåll* as a heading not only for the table of Contents [*sic*] of his books (e.g., Gustaf Aulén, *Kristen gudstro i förändringens värld: en studie,* Stockholm: Diakonistyrelsens, 1967, p. [i]; elsewhere, *Innehållsförteckning,* as in his major work, *Den allmänneliga kristna tron,* 5te upplagan, Stockholm: Svenska Kyrkans Diakonistyrelses, 1957, p. 418), but as a salient heading also for his theology of faith. He uses the term with *tro* (faith) not only in the course of much of his writing (e.g., *trons innehåll.* in the former of the two works just cited, p. 36) but also as an explicit and virtually central theme (e.g., in the latter). The over-all title of all those parts of this latter work other than the Introduction is *Det kristna trosinnehållet* (Christian faith-content: p. [109]), in the Introduction he having devoted one section (§ 6) to the topic *Trons innehåll* (content of faith) (pp. 67-75) and its first sub-section to *Tro och trosinnehåll* (faith and faith-content) (pp. 68-71) (cf. also § 7, pp. 75 ff.) In the influential English translation all this comes out as "The Content of Christian Faith", "The Content of Faith", "Faith and the Content of Faith" (pp. [115], 73 [five times], 77, 78, 79 ff.: cf. [table of] Contents, p. [iii]); occasionally the definite article appears, "the Content of the [*sic*] Christian Faith" (p. 79). Gustaf Aulén, *The Faith of the Christian Church,* translated from the fourth Swedish edition by Eric H. Wahlstrom and G. Everett Arden, Philadelphia: Muhlenberg, 1948. (I have no reason to suppose that in this matter of titles, between the fourth Swedish edition from which the translators were working and the fifth, the only one accessible to me, there was significant divergence. In the text itself, there are some significant additions and modifications in the later Swedish, I notice.) He affirms that (Christian) faith has a definite (*fast och bestämt*—p. 68; cf. also p. 67) content (although this is qualified by "in principle"— English, p. 73 *bis*, 74; *principiellt sett*, p. 68; cf. *principiellt*, pp. 67, 68). This content of faith is given it by divine revelation (Swedish, p. 67; English, p. 73). He uses the phrasings explicitly differentiating his understanding from, on the one hand, "intellectual" (pp. 74-75; *intellektualistiska*,pp. 68-70) interpretations of faith (which make content primary, he says) and, on the other, from "subjective" (pp. 74, 75-77; *subjektivistiska*, pp. 68, 70-71) (which make it secondary). Stressing, in passing, more the will of God (*gudsviljan*, p. 58; English, p. 73) than propositions in revelation, he concludes that "the content of faith is in reality nothing else than the God who reveals Himself" (English, p. 77; *Trons innehåll är nämligen intet annat än den sig uppenbarande Guden*; p. 71). Here, then, "content" of faith converges with what others classically call faith's object. (He does not seem to reckon with the problem of how, if the content be God, it/He can then be *fast och bestämt* rather than transcendent.)

To the identification of belief with the "content" of faith, I personally prefer, if one is at all to use that to me infelicitous term, the French Catholic thinker Jacques Maritain's reverse observation. He notes that what I would call propositional belief—or indeed, propositional knowledge, even, regarded as "purely intellectual information"— risks in modern times being regarded as "normal" in religious life while in fact, far from being itself the content of faith, it "tends indeed to empty faith of its content". Similarly all second-hand believing (even on the testimony of the Church) that is not a *seeing*—in our terms: whatever is belief rather than recognition—"again . . . leads . . . to emptying faith of its content". These remarks are taken from an address entitled "The Ways [*sic*] of Faith", first given presumably in French (to the "Semaine des intellectuels catholiques", Paris, May 8, 1949) but a French version, or reference to a published French version, is not available to me; so that I do not know if *contenu* was used. The article was published in English in *The Commonweal*, 51: No. 1 (Nov. 4, 1949), 87-93, and reprinted thence in slightly revised form in the expanded English collection, Jacques Maritain, *The Range of Reason*, New York: Scribner's, 1952, and London: Geoffrey Bles, 1953 (the two passages cited in both cases: pp. 208, 209; the wording in *The Commonweal*, p. 89, varies slightly): the French version does not, of course (cf. dates), appear in the smaller original of this: Jacques Maritain, *Raison et raisons: essais détachés*, Paris: Librairie Universelle de France, 1947. (Some of the articles included in the enlarged English version were written originally in English; if this one was first composed in French, as seems probable, the revised translation was done by the author with perhaps the help of Mrs. Pierre Brodin [p. ix].)

If, as seems probable, the phrase "content of faith" came into English from the Continent (originally from Hegel?), then we may note that the German word *Inhalt* (also *Gehalt*) has non-empirical connotations far more generously than does the French term *contenu* or even English "content" (although of the English term this nuance seems to have been felt more in earlier centuries than during the twentieth, and to obtain in its use in literary and art criticism more than in philosophy or theology). The German terms constitute the standard vernacular equivalent of the scholastic *substantia*, as appears in the phrases *Inhalt und Form, Gehalt und Form*. More strikingly, the suggestion of implication, over against what is explicit or specific, specified, becomes clear in the phrase *etwas dem Inhalt und Buchstaben nach ehren*, "to honour something in spirit and in letter", and generally in the adverbial usages *dem Inhalte nach, inhaltlich, in inhalt-licher Beziehung*, which may be rendered "virtually" or the like (or: "substantially"). The reference is to what is covert or implied or subtle. In this sense, *der Inhalt des*

Glaubens could mean that to which faith's propositions point. In our terms, beliefs would determine the form of faith, as distinct from its substance.

For the table that lists chapter-headings of a book the Germans use *Inhalt*, the French *Table des matières*. On this point, English sides with German, admittedly. It is interesting to reflect on how far in the German here the reference is to the topics being treated, in the French manner of the phrasing, and how far rather to the treatment of them, in the English. The former case leaves open a possibility that these topics may, and presumably do, transcend what is said about them within the book. My knowledge of Swedish is far too superficial to comment on its counterpart term *innehåll*; I am told that its connotation is strongly of a container containing something. (Especially would this be so, of course, when it is used with an epithet like *fast och bestämt*.) It would make a difference in understanding Aulén, however, if one translated him as writing of "the substance of faith". So far as German is concerned, it would perhaps hardly be too far-fetched to suggest that *der Inhalt* comes as close to the English term "subject" as it does to "object".

The notion that faith does, should, or can have a "content" deserves more scrutiny than it has yet, to my knowledge, had.

45. Schleiermacher, *Glaube*, esp. chap. I.

46. "Contours of Faith" is the title of a recent work by Dillenberger. One of its chapters, moreover, is entitled "The Shape of Faith"; and one of its sections, "The Form of Faith". "Forms of faith", "ways of faith" and "modes of faith" are used in an English translation of Rahner: the original has chiefly *Gestalt* (Rahner speaks, even, of *die verschiedensten Gestalten des Glaubens*); also, *Weise und Gestalt*. A great many other examples of these and also of other terms could be cited--especially of "forms of faith", increasingly used by many modern writers, including me. I also affect "patterns of faith". The phrase "structure of faith" figures in the sub-title of the English translation of one of the more deeply personalist of modern French Catholic writers, Mouroux. In the current version of the original, the phrase *structure personnelle de la foi* is found in the course of the text, but is proffered guardedly, almost apologetically, and it is not found on the title-page. Evidently in this case (contrast or compare Cullmann above, our ref. 43) the author has been dissuaded from continuing to give it prominence, whether by internal second thoughts or by outside pressure one can only speculate; for apparently (although I have not succeeded in locating copies) earlier editions did display this wording as sub-title. The American theologian Cobb elects also the currently fashionable word "structure", but does not go on to speak of "faith"—that word evidently having in our day already moved for him too far, presumably in the direction along which "belief" has already long since moved for most of the rest of us. He speaks, accordingly, not of "Buddhist faith" or "Christian faith", but rather of "Buddhist existence" and "Christian existence".

John Dillenberger, *Contours of Faith: Changing Forms of Christian Thought,* Nashville and New York: Abingdon, 1969 (cf. p. 83); Karl Rahner, *Im Heute glauben,* Einsiedeln: Benziger, 1965 (Hans Küng, ed., Theologische Meditationen, No. 9), *passim*: e.g., pp. 7, 9, 10, 11; Karl Rahner, *Faith Today*, Ray and Rosaleen Ockenden, transs., London and Melbourne: Sheed and Ward, 1967, *passim*: e.g., pp. 4, 5. J. Mouroux, *I Believe: The Personal Structure of Faith*, trans. Michael Turner, New York: Sheed and Ward, 1959. Jean Mouroux, *Je crois en toi: la rencontre avec le Dieu vivant,* Paris, Éditions du Cerf, 1965 (Collection *Foi vivante*); the cited passage is p. 107 (the original reads in full, as opening sentence of the short concluding chapter: "L'esquisse trop rapide qu'on vient de lire aura sans doute montré à quel point il est juste de parler d'*une structure personnelle de la foi"* [italics original].) *"Biblio" 1949: catalogue des ouvrages parus en langue française dans le monde entier,* Paris: Hachette, 1951 (vol. 16) carries the following entry (p. 560): Mouroux, Jean. *Je crois en toi. Structure personnelle de la foi* (Coll. Foi vivante) . . . '49 Editions de la Revue des jeunes. *Extr. des Recherches de science religieuse, 1938;* and *"Biblio" 1954* (Paris, 1955: vol. 21), p. 571, enters a second edition with the same wording, this time with Éditions du Cerf as publisher. My copy of the 1965 edition of the Mouroux work gives 1965 as the copyright date and makes no acknowledgement of earlier versions. John B. Cobb, Jr., *The Structure of Christian Existence,* Philadelphia: Westminster, 1967; for "Buddhist Existence", see p. 60.

47. *Summa Theologiae,* IIa IIae, qu. 1, esp. art. 1; cf. artt. 5-9 and qu. 2, artt. 5-8. (Lethielleux edn., vol. III, pp. 1-24, 28-33.) On this matter cf. also my *Faith & Belief,* chap. 5.

General Index

Index of Biblical Passages

Index of Some Significant
Hebrew and Greek Terms